MURDER IN
BATTLE CREEK

MURDER IN
BATTLE CREEK

The Mysterious Death of Daisy Zick

BLAINE L. PARDOE

Foreword by David B. Schock of DelayedJustice.com

Charleston   London

THE
History
PRESS

Published by The History Press
Charleston, SC 29403
www.historypress.net

Copyright © 2013 by Blaine L. Pardoe
All rights reserved

First published 2013

Manufactured in the United States

ISBN 978.1.62619.134.1

Library of Congress CIP data applied for.

To my wife, Cyndi, who puts up with my writing and gives me encouragement even when she doesn't realize it. To my kids, Alexander and Victoria—and my grandson Trenton—you never know where the information will take you. To my mom, Rose Pardoe, who has been anxiously waiting for me to finish this book. Finally to Central Michigan University, my alma mater.

CONTENTS

FOREWORD

S omebody knows something. Somebody *always* knows something."
   The speaker was Jim Fairbanks, a retired detective who had served his
career with the Holland Police Department (HPD). Jim had worked for decades
with that department and had—long before our conversation—headed the
city's efforts to solve the 1979 abduction and strangulation of Janet Chandler.
By the time I spoke with him in 2003, he was long off the job and had a lot
of time to think about the case, which just would not be solved. This was the
case that kept the members—current and former—of the HPD up at nights,
wondering. Above all else, Jim was certain that somebody knew something
about the crime; it hadn't happen in a vacuum. And it was his certainty that
helped to drive us to share the story of Janet's murder in the documentary
Who Killed Janet Chandler? (For more about this, please see my website, www.
delayedjustice.com.)

   Over the intervening years, I have quoted Jim again and again. Almost
always, somebody does know something. In most murder cases, somebody
has either witnessed something relevant or listened to someone talk about
the event, perhaps voiced in a threat or a confession. We believe that most
often somebody besides the killer knows what happened.

   And sometimes as a result continued prodding, the truth will come out.
Geoffrey Chaucer, in the "Nun's Priest's Tale" of *The Canterbury Tales*, put it
this way: "Murder will out that we see day by day."

   We do. And it's marvelous when that happens. In this day and age, we
see great strides in solving murders from decades before, thanks to the

employment of new technologies, DNA chief among them. Sometimes it's just dogged determination, even when there is no forensic evidence. Many departments have devoted the time of senior detectives to what they are calling cold case units. Other agencies have convened interdepartmental task forces. The results have been both stunning and welcome.

But not every case responds to such an approach. So far, for instance, the 1963 murder of Daisy Zick has been stubbornly resistant. And now it falls to the historian to have a shot at retelling one of the most baffling of all Michigan murders.

Blaine Lee Pardoe is a historian who publishes prolifically. He's also a very friendly and approachable person, someone you actually could—and would want to—talk with. He and I met in the fall of 2011, when each of us was receiving an award from the Historical Society of Michigan: he for his book *Lost Eagles: One Man's Mission to Find Mission Airmen in Two World Wars* and I for my film about Detroit's Poet Laureate, *Star by Star: Naomi Long Madgett, Poet & Publisher.* Blaine's book offered a careful telling of the story of Frederick Zinn, a man who devoted his life to bringing home the remains of lost American airmen. Along the way, Zinn developed techniques that would serve all searchers. The book had been published by the University of Michigan Press and was a lovely example of fine work between an author and a publisher.

If that had been Blaine's sole contribution, it would have been enough. But as we chatted that evening, I learned that he had done so much more, including a then-forthcoming book about a murder, *Secret Witness: The Untold Story of the 1967 Bombing in Marshall, Michigan,* another University of Michigan collaboration. And there was another murder book in the works after that: this one.

Well, three books doth an author make.

But Blaine had written so very many more. As I was to find out later, there are more than sixty titles to his name, and they deal with military history, true crime, computers, games and gaming and business management. And then there are all the online publications and nearly countless articles; he's a veritable polymath. He says he has a life other than writing and gives credit to his wife, Cyndi; children, Victoria and Alexander; and grandson, Trenton. He also has a day job.

So when I was asked to write this introduction, I jumped at the chance. The reason first and foremost was that I'd have a chance to read the book before you did; I was eager. Beyond that, it's nice to have something to do with highly productive people; they are different from the rest of us. And finally, I might have an opportunity to assert to readers that Blaine's work with worthy of support and encouragement.

And what a subject he's chosen this time.

Unsolved homicides can be difficult to chronicle, especially those that I call "delayed justice" cases, the old and cold. (Believe me, there is nothing "cold" about a murder to a family member of a victim; it is always present and current.) This is a case that is now fifty years beyond the event. It's possible, perhaps even likely, that the killer has gone to his (or her, as Blaine points out) final accounting. And the records may be there but likely are in some ways incomplete or deficient. And many who took part in the investigations and who could have filled in the missing pieces have gone on as well.

But just because the case is from a bygone era doesn't mean that it might not be solved. Time is not always the enemy of truth. People age and change. Sometimes they grow courageous or refuse to be further intimidated; sometimes they find religion or faith. Sometimes those who once terrified them die, and the carriers of knowledge are freed from the oppression of fear. They may marry, divorce, have children or even grandchildren. Or, on their deathbeds, the murderers or those who know about the murders may want to clear a guilty conscience. The future is always unknowable, and any number of things can and do happen that lead to the result that "murder will out."

Blaine has employed his skills as a writer and his training as a historian and combined them with the healthy imagination he displays in his fiction to give us an honest and unvarnished reporting of the fate of Daisy Zick.

Blaine makes no pretense of his qualifications: "I'm an author and historian; not a detective."

Well, yes and no.

Any good historian is something of a detective. There is the drive to find the real answers to unknowns, the desire to fill in the blanks. Any solid historian shares that vital curiosity with a good detective. I suspect what he means is something other—that he doesn't think like a sworn officer of the law; he thinks differently.

It's good to bring that kind of outside thinking to a murder investigation. Police have told me as much. And they've also told me that sometimes our associates—researchers and others with special skills—add to the strengths of the team looking for answers. One officer once told me, "Doc, you have some interesting friends." He was referring to a professor of forensic psychiatry and a graphoanalyst whom I'd asked to consult on a case. Blaine also brings his own team.

And then there are the readers, who are also self-selecting members of a broader team. There is always the possibility that a reader will discover a connection to a crime that had been previously unknown.

Even I fall into this category for this book. Only three years after the murder, I enrolled at Albion College, a small liberal arts college not too far from Battle Creek. One of my classmates was Ken Zick. Ken had family in the area. My supposition is that Daisy may have married into a branch of his family. (Ken has more recently said he was unaware of either a Daisy Zick or the Daisy Zick murder; he's now investigating, too.)

But you don't have to have a connection to this murder to find it interesting. It remains, after all, a great unknown, something of a rarity of the time. In the first place, it was a suburban murder, and those, according to statistics from the U.S. Department of Justice, accounted for a little more than 7 percent (610) of all murders in the United States (8,640) in 1963. (By comparison there were 14,748 murders in 2010.)

Daisy Zick's murder was one of only 283 in Michigan in 1963. (That compares with 567 in 2010; the highest number was 1,186 in 1974.) Moreover, it was one of very few unsolved homicides. In 1963, more than 91 percent of all homicides were cleared by arrests or other extraordinary means. And that's a far better percentage than the 64 percent clearance rate in the United States in 2008. The rate is far lower than that in Michigan; the Michigan State Police in the Michigan Incident Crime Reporting publication put the 2011 clearance rate at 24 percent. I have talked with a statistician at the Michigan State Police who said they are trying to find the reason for the drop. A few years earlier, we had been the lowest in the nation with a 52 percent clearance rate. What a 24 percent rate means is anybody's best guess. It would seem that you'd have better than a three-out-of-four chance of getting away with murder here. I hope those figures are open to correction, and an upward correction at that. Such a low rate is unsettling, if not deeply distressing for me at least. But then, I take a very dim view of murder; it's a bad idea, a very bad idea. It violates every precept that's been handed down to us as a standard for right living. It is an offense against God and man. This intentional depravation of the one thing that ought to be ours—our lives—strikes at the root of a just society.

And yet it happens. And sometimes the killers get away with it.

And sometimes people write books about it or make films or tell stories. We recognize that there is value in retelling the story—it should not be lost to our shared history. And it should stand out because it represents a break from our usual way of going about life, trusting that we can walk out our front doors in safety or relying on fragile glass to keep the outside world outside. In the event of a murder, there is something that upsets the right order. And that jars some of us, people such as Blaine and me and a host of others.

12

But there are ways of going about it that might be helpful and those that might not be. As Blaine puts it, "Armchair quarterbacking of murders is easy and dangerously seductive to undertake."

Blaine has not been seduced by the easy answer or the innocent wonderment of it all. He digs deep, speaking with as many people who were around and know the victims and putative suspects.

And he does one other thing I deeply appreciate: he takes the time to look into the backgrounds of the investigators. You will know the circumstances of their lives, their families, the way they speak and their fates. Blaine realizes that each of them left indelible impressions on this case and that those impressions remain. And he notes that, in their way, they also suffered because the crime remains unsolved.

Daisy Zick's life and that of her husband, Floyd, is laid bare. We know of her serial affairs and that possibility that she may have had several going on at one time. We know of Floyd's infidelities as well and his predilection to drink. But we also know something of their care for each other; somehow, their marriage worked. And we know that Daisy was a meticulous person in all she did. Had she lived, it's possible she might have been a very prim little old lady with a tidy house that had everything in its place.

Blaine is not cruel in his revelations of her personal life, a life that must be examined in the context of her murder. He does not make sport of anyone's failings in this book. The book manages to be interesting without any hint of the salacious. And there is even humor, but not of the gallows' kind. And while Blaine is an entertaining fellow, that is not his sole purpose here. He—like most historians—is a lover of order. Murder succeeds in disorder.

And he is a lover of transparency and revelation. Murder festers in secrecy.

In short, Blaine has taken up arms in this effort for the restoration of a broken order. Daisy Zick is important—as important today as she ever was—and her unsolved murder calls out for solution, resolution and a reordering of history. This telling of her story is an important work, and I commend Blaine and his writing to your attention.

In Micah 6:8 of the English Standard Bible, we are called to our work: "He has told you, O man, what is good; and what does the Lord require of you but to do justice, and to love kindness, and to walk humbly with your God?"

DAVID B. SCHOCK, PHD

David B. Schock, PhD, is a writer and filmmaker. His films about unsolved homicides include Who Killed Janet Chandler?, Finding Diane, Jack in the Box, Into the Dark, The Heritage Hill Bride *and* Murder on the Third Floor *(the last two primary documentaries). In addition, he maintains a website, www.delayedjustice. com, that chronicles hundreds of Michigan murders. His most recent book is* Judicial Deceit: Tyranny and Unnecessary Secrecy at the Michigan Supreme Court *(with coauthor Chief Justice Elizabeth A. Weaver [retired]). In addition, he is an active musician.*

ACKNOWLEDGEMENTS

One must never set up a murder. They must happen unexpectedly, as in life.
Alfred Hitchcock

When you try to reconstruct a crime that is half a century old and unsolved, it can be challenging to say the least. One of the challenges I faced was whether I should use the real names of the people involved or substitute them with pseudonyms. I opted to use the real names of individuals. My reasons for this are twofold.

First, I obtained the case file via a Freedom of Information Act request and countless interviews, as can anyone with the money and time. While people's accounts were never validated under oath, their names and what they said are a matter of public record. The mentioning of a name in this book implies nothing more than that the person was, in some way, involved with the investigation or talked to by the authorities during it.

Second, this remains an open murder case. The use of real names may yet trigger memories and generate tips or leads that can lead police to close the case.

I am an author, not a detective. I approached the massive case file differently than a police officer would have. There are things I dug into, such as Daisy's past, which an investigator in the case might not have. I don't have any delusions about being the one to solve the case. My role here is to present the story as best I can, and I have tried to keep the focus solely on the details and facts that seemed pertinent to me in telling this story.

Solving this case, well, that is up to you. It won't be solved by me as the author but by someone coming forward with new information and by good investigators who act on that information.

ACKNOWLEDGEMENTS

Finally, there are some accounts of people who were there that are impossible to reconcile with the documented case file. In some instances, memories are off with people; in others, the detail in the case file simply isn't there. I have done my best to present the most accurate account of what happened starting on January 14, 1963. I apologize in advance if any minor mistakes were made.

I would like to thank the following people for their help. My apologies to any I may have missed:

Jim King—Daisy's son. Jim provided me with a great deal of information on his mother and stepfather.
Dick Stevens—Dick is an icon in the legal circle of Calhoun County. His memories of events and people are remarkable.
Jean Armstrong—my intrepid researcher and genealogist helped a great deal.
Janet Arlt
Roy Bechtol
David Calhoun
Trace Christenson
Panda Englerth, Hastings Public Library
Myrtle Evans
John Hazard Forbes
Judy Fox, Assistant FOIA Coordinator, Michigan State Police
Toni A. Fritz, Chief Deputy Circuit Court Clerk, Thirty-seventh Circuit Court Clerk's Office
Mary Diane Hawkins, Assistant Librarian, Hastings Public Library
Gary Hough
Georgialee Huettl
Dorothy Kajcienski
Ralph Kartheu
Sharon McIntyre
Mary McMillen
Susan K. Mladenoff, Prosecuting Attorney, Calhoun County
Jody Owens
Lynnette Rich
Fred Ritchie
Wayne Rizor
Tom Sanders
Marie (Fales) Tungate
Carla Turner, Assistant FOIA Coordinator, Michigan State Police

So now, it is time to turn the clock back to January 1963 outside the city of Battle Creek Michigan.

INTRODUCTION

People always ask me, "Where do you get your ideas for books you write?" The reality is that most ideas come to me as opposed to me looking for them. I either stumble across them while writing another book, or someone makes a casual suggestion to me that "this might be worth looking into." Daisy Zick came to me in such a way, and she led me down many interesting twists and turns along the way. The more I dug into the case files, the more I came to respect the investigators and was intrigued with the story that began to emerge.

Daisy Zick's case came to my attention in 2009. I was working on my book on the 1967 bombing murder in Marshall, Michigan, titled *Secret Witness*. When I was doing research on *Secret Witness*, I would sometimes be vague with people asking what I was working on by saying, "I'm doing a book about a 1960s murder in Calhoun County." Inevitably they would say, "Ah, you must be talking about the Daisy Zick case." After the third time this happened, I started asking questions about that case as well as the one I was researching. The more questions I asked, the more fascinating the story became.

I tend to favor writing about crimes that are not recent, and this fit that bill, having occurred over fifty years ago. While memories are blurred, people are now able to be more open in their discussions about the case. The fear that the murderer might strike back at them after all this time has faded—for some at least. It allowed people to be brutally honest in what they thought and said.

The crime surprised me because it happened in my childhood neighborhood in Emmett Township outside Battle Creek. In fact, Daisy

Zick's home, where the crime took place, is within walking distance of the elementary school I attended only a few years later. I delivered newspapers in my youth to the home where her car was abandoned by the murderer. Daisy's murder was the first in decades that remained unsolved in Calhoun County, making it a rarity.

In 1963, murders were less common in Calhoun County than today, and they almost always got resolved, usually quickly. Prior to Daisy Zick's murder, there were only two other unsolved murders in the area. William Smith had been shot on Hamblin Avenue, and Estelle Terry had been killed in the Bailey Park neighborhood during World War II. Until the 1960s, the concept of cold cases that remained unsolved was foreign. Now, unsolved cases are far too commonplace, a sad indication of our times.

Daisy's murder captured my attention because of its viciousness and the fact that, at the time of this writing, the crime remained unsolved, at least as far as the public knew. I discovered that some of the investigators thought they had found the guilty parties over the decades and that the case was solved in some of their minds if not in a court of law. Only in the minds and fading memories of the citizens of Battle Creek, Michigan, does the murder still linger like a nagging nightmare. Most people are unaware of just how close investigators came to resolution of this crime.

Daisy's death was exceedingly brutal. She was beaten about the head and viciously stabbed over twenty times. Her death was premeditated. Her killer cut the phone cord in the home, traveled from a distance on one of the coldest days of the year and committed the crime in broad daylight. Despite there being several witnesses when the murderer fled the scene, no one has been formally charged with the crime.

The rumors tied to the Daisy Zick killing were ingrained into the collective memories of Battle Creek. There were stories circulating of her "little black book," which allegedly listed the men that she had slept with. Marriages were said to be shattered as a result of her killing and the investigation that followed. Daisy is often portrayed both as victim and culprit. Variations of the events tied to this crime were spread from generation to generation, each new retelling corrupting the story a little bit more. Dozens of theories surfaced over the years as suspicious neighbors came up with their own ideas as to who committed the murder and why. The Daisy Zick story became a local legend, a bit of the mythology of Battle Creek.

Daisy worked at the Kellogg Company, one of the largest employers in Calhoun County and the company that put Battle Creek, Michigan, on America's map. Like all large corporate entities, it had its own culture. Kellogg's was like a social community within the larger Battle Creek society. It had its own grapevine, its own rumors, its own dark side that seems to evade company annual reports. Everyone working there knew Daisy in some way, and within that tight little community in the brick-walled factory, they helped feed the story of who might have killed her and why.

I had a chance to meet with some of the men who worked the Zick case over the years. While most of them have long since retired, I learned the truth in the old adage that there is no such thing as an ex-cop. Most of them, just like I did, wanted the final justice, some sort of closure on Daisy's murder. At the same time, some were quick to point out that Daisy's extramarital affairs contributed to her case not being solved. Their words echoed the sentiments of a number of people whom I interviewed: Daisy's lifestyle in some way made her party to her own death. Somehow, her infidelity was what brought about her death. This insensitivity to Daisy was unearned and unwarranted. No one deserves what she went through in the last moments of her life or to be brutally murdered and have her killer walk free.

When I posted on Facebook and my blog that I was working on this book, I was stunned as people confided to me new tips and leads for the crime. Hundreds of people read my blog entries about the crime. Phone calls and emails started coming in, some with theories, some with actual tips. I had to reach out to the state police and provide them the leads, though they have not indicated whether any have panned out yet. What this told me was that people were still excited and interested in this murder. People love a good mystery, and this case certainly is one.

The original investigation was botched by today's standards. Mistakes were made, not deliberately but because the nature of this murder was so far beyond the capabilities of local law enforcement. Making matters worse was the political infighting among some of the agencies and entities involved. As I pored over the case file, I saw that the investigation seemed sloppy and misdirected, the result of an age when police work was interviewing people and trusting experience and instincts. The 1963 limitations of criminal science hindered what the investigators could learn through science. A great deal of the evidence from the crime is still held in a vault at the Michigan State Police headquarters. Perhaps a new examination of it, using modern techniques, might provide new directions.

The investigation of this case seemed to pass on to newer generations of investigators, who brought new insights, perspectives and desire to resolve the murder. With each new generation that took on the hunt for the killer came tantalizing leads that all seemed to fizzle. Ultimately, as late as 2001, investigators found themselves walking down the same path their colleagues had done in 1963.

In looking at this as a potential book, I was nervous because the crime is still unsolved. Many true-crime authors steer clear of such projects for all the obvious reasons. People want to see a book like this driven to the end. They want answers, a sense of closure. With an unsolved crime, some of those things are not achievable. There was a time when I considered not writing this book for these reasons. Two books changed that for me: Mardi Link's *When Evil Came to Good Hart* and Mark Fuhrman's *Murder in Greenwich: Who Killed Martha Moxley?*

Link wrote her book about an unsolved Michigan killing in the same decade as the Zick murder. From it, I saw that such a book was possible and found a way to provide readers with a chance to come to their own conclusions given the suspects involved. Regardless of what you think of Mark Fuhrman and his involvement in the O.J. Simpson Case, his prying open the case on Martha Moxley led to an arrest and eventual conviction of her killer. I came to realize that a trial and conviction were not necessary for a great book about a true crime. In fact, shedding light on the open wound the community felt might just bring out new details and new clues that could help bring a real end to the case.

Daisy only had one child, Jim King. I have met with Jim and talked with him on the phone on several occasions. When you look into his face and hear his voice, you come to understand one thing: he has never stopped loving his mother. Despite the decades that have passed, he has never stopped wanting some degree of closure. Someone killed his mother, and the investigation seems to have halted. When he spoke, I didn't hear or see an older gentleman in front of me, but I saw, instead, a young boy who loved his mother very deeply. Other than Jim and his family, there is no one in the wings whispering Daisy's name, taking up her cause and prodding officials to find long-hidden answers. There is no one other than total strangers, such as myself and a handful of police officers, that is still searching for that elusive justice she so rightly deserves. The only other people that want to know are the people of Battle Creek who view this murder as an old wound that occasionally opens and bleeds into the history of the city.

Now nearly half century has passed since that bitter cold January morning when Daisy was savagely beaten, tied up and stabbed. The key suspects are dead. If one of them was not the murderer, the true killer most likely has

Emmett Township, Wattles Park Michigan

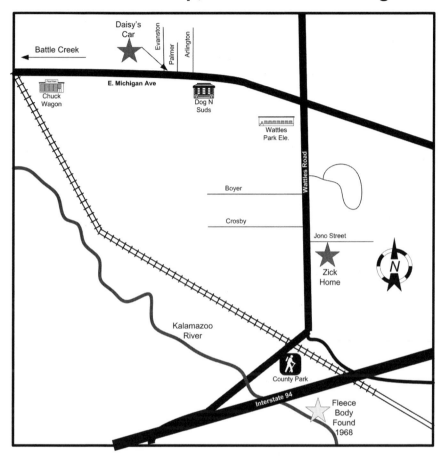

passed away by now. But there's no statute of limitations in Michigan for murder. There is a chance, however slim, that someone reading this book knows something, perhaps a rumor that grew from some kernel of truth decades earlier, that might shed new light on this crime. It's not too late to bring solace to Daisy Zick.

Chapter 1
DAISY'S LAST DAY ALIVE

She was nice to everyone. I never heard her say a bad word about anyone. If she didn't like a person she would leave them alone but would never say anything about them.
Battle Creek Enquirer and News
January 14, 1963

When you speak to anyone about the day of Daisy Zick's murder—Tuesday, January 14, 1963—they almost always start by telling you about weather. It was cold, bitterly cold, even by mid-Michigan standards. The night before the murder the temperature was near zero. The day Daisy died, it was going to dip to between ten to seventeen degrees below zero after nightfall. There was already six inches of snow on the ground, and the forecast called for another two by the evening. Gusting breezes made the cold penetrate even the warmest coat and nostrils sting just to breathe. Mustaches became white and brittle with frost in a matter of minutes. Gunmetal-gray skies unleashed a stinging snow that day, making it that much more undesirable to be out. Caught in the twenty-five-mile-per-hour wind gusts, the fine powder drifted as it hit the already snow-covered ground. The snow was the kind that crunched and squeaked loudly under the soles of boots. It seemed odd that someone would pick such a day for a murder since the weather was bound to keep people at home. Then again, there were a lot of things that didn't add up about the crime that day.

Daisy did not have an inkling that January 14, 1963, was going to be the last morning of her life. It was supposed to be a normal day, almost mundane, even by Battle Creek standards. For her, that day was supposed to be another

One of the last known photographs of Daisy Zick. *Courtesy of the Battle Creek Historical Society.*

day on the factory floor. She was most likely looking forward to a cup of coffee with a friend before heading off to her afternoon shift on a production line in the packing department at the Kellogg Factory in Battle Creek. Daisy was an attractive, forty-three-year-old redhead. People who knew her described her as "peppy," "outgoing," "friendly" and "perky." She was short, only five foot two, with a slender .108-pound body.

Daisy and her husband, Floyd, lived in the modest suburb of Calhoun County's Battle Creek called Emmett Township, specifically in Wattles Park. Calhoun County, Michigan, is one that is a mix of contradictions and as such, it struggles with the image that it wanted to portray. Much of the county is rural, with the flat Goguac Plains growing corn and wheat for the burgeoning breakfast cereal industry. But there is also a distinctly industrial edge to the county. Battle Creek was a factory town whose primary business was to put meals on the world's kitchen tables every morning. The Kellogg Company and Post Cereals plants were only a block apart, separated by a strip of seedy bars and tiny lunch restaurants. The county had tiny, unbelievably quaint little towns, like Marshall, which appeared to have been the backdrop of a Norman Rockwell painting, and Albion, Michigan, with its red brick roads and a grittier look and feel to it. Compared to the tall buildings of Battle Creek, the smaller communities stood out. Battle Creek was the industrial hub of the county, while the other towns clung to old traditions and ideals.

Part of what made Calhoun County successful was its positioning between Chicago and Detroit, right on Interstate 94 and the railroad lines. During

World War II, the county had sprouted several boom businesses, like Eaton's, that made parts for the war effort. This brought in an influx of people from the south, who came north looking for work. Calhoun County accepted these newcomers.

The Zick home was a small brown brick, ranch-style house in Emmett Township just outside Battle Creek's city limit. The township had originally been named Milton, but by 1840, the State of Michigan had figured out that it had three townships by that name. It renamed the township after the Irish patriot Robert Emmet who fought the English for Ireland's independence despite the fact that there were few people of Irish decent living in the area.

For years the township was a farming community. A pole-supported bridge was erected over the Kalamazoo River at one end of the township, which helped foster the wheat production and travel in the area. The bridge was purchased by Citizen's Electric Light Company, which erected an iron bridge on the site in 1908. The wheat fields were renamed "County Park" and soon became a common place for teenagers to make out. In the summers, kids swung from thick ropes out over the Kalamazoo River for a cooling swim. Families picnicked in the park near the spring-fed creek that twisted from the tunnel under the railroad embankment to the river. County Park was easy walking distance from the Zick home.

The hope had always been that Emmett Township would evolve into a town on its own right, but it never seemed to emerge from the shadow of Battle Creek. One of the largest subdivisions of the township was Wattles Park. It had been named after Dr. Jervis Wattles, one of the first physicians in Battle Creek.

Like Emmett Township, Wattles Park had aspirations of being a true community on its own but struggled with a lack of a business center that people could gravitate around. Instead it emerged as a suburb of Battle Creek, small- to medium-sized homes for the factory workers of Battle Creek. Not quite as upscale as Lakeview but not as urban as Pennfield, Wattles Park was often thought of as being at the edge of farm country. The suburb was a mix of suburb, farming community and business district, each negating the others for dominance. Like many suburbs, it struggled to find an identity.

Where Wattles Road intersected Michigan Avenue was more of a sleepy crossroads, the kind of place that was easy to miss as you drove between Marshall and Battle Creek. Wattles Park had a cluster of tiny stores at a blinking light that marked the hub of commerce. There was a wood-floored grocery store (Steve's) that predated modern convenience stores. It was a place where pop, candy or staples could be purchased. Mr. Laverne Chase had built a popular local soda bar at the intersection, but by 1963, it had been sold and turned into Jalisco's Mexican Restaurant, better known as Emilio's, one of the few such establishments in the area. Hoff's Hardware was situated there along with Walter's Electrical Service, Keelan's Barber Shop and Hoff's Service Station.

At the time, Wattles Park barely merited a reference on road maps. It was a quiet community, almost invisible to the outside world. People knew their neighbors but kept to themselves. Kids rode their bikes along the roads with little fear of accidents. The Wattles Park Men's Club sponsored children's baseball and softball at the nearby elementary school. This was not the place where killers stalked the streets. This was a slice of semirural America.

The Zicks lived on a dead-end road called Juno Street, which was off Wattles Road a block from Wattles Park Junior High that was planned to open that year and a half-mile from Wattles Park Elementary. They lived less than a mile from the intersection at Wattles Road and Michigan Avenue, the business heart of the area. The elementary school was within a hundred yards of the Wattles Park crossroads, and its presence was the one thing that gave the suburb any sense of community. Many of the children coming or going to school walked right past Juno Street every day. In 1963, if you lived within a half mile of school, you were expected to walk, and that was the kind of community it was. It was also the kind of community where strangers stood out. On the biting cold day of January 14, most of the children were heavily bundled against the biting wind and snow. They didn't notice anything out of the ordinary, or at least that was what they would tell police later. Their focus was to get to their respective schools and get warm.

Daisy's morning unfolded as it had hundreds of times before. Her husband, Floyd, left earlier in the morning than she did, around 7:45 a.m., to go to his job at Fales' Market, where he worked as a butcher, about four miles from his home. When he left for work, he woke up his wife, as he did every morning. Floyd stopped and picked up a co-worker, Florence Van Uun, five minutes later. He drove her to work every day, and she later noted that there was nothing different about that morning. The folks that worked at Fales' Market were a tight-knit family. They celebrated Christmas parties together and knew one another on a personal level. It was the kind of small business where you didn't just know the employee, you knew their spouses and what sports or after school activities their kids were involved with.

Daisy worked the afternoon shift at Kellogg's. Her seat was at the end of one of the packaging station's production lines near the main aisle, so anyone walking through the factory would inevitably pass by her. The seat that she had was one that rotated, but there was no privacy. "Daisy worked out in the open, very public. Everyone that walked through knew her," was a comment one of her co-workers made. Her personality was so outgoing that she was widely recognized in the factory.

This Tuesday, Daisy planned to meet her friend and co-worker Audrey Heminger of Vicksburg, Michigan, at Vello's Restaurant, a quaint bar and restaurant on East Columbia Avenue at Main Street. They were scheduled to meet between 10:00 and 10:30 a.m. for a cup of coffee together. From there, she would go to the plant a mile or so away to take her seat on the packaging line. Other than the biting cold outside, it was to be a typical day for Daisy. If anything out of the ordinary was expected, it certainly didn't reflect in her plans for the day or the evidence in her home.

It seemed to be a slow news day for the rest of the country. The top song in the nation was "Go Away Little Girl," by Steve Lawrence. The Bijou Theater in downtown Battle Creek was showing the film *In Search of the Castaways*, a Disney film starring Hayley Mills and Maurice Chevalier. George Wallace was getting sworn in as governor of Alabama that day, giving his now-infamous "segregation today, segregation tomorrow, segregation forever" speech. In Michigan, the speech didn't even warrant coverage in the newspapers except for a small article buried in the *Battle Creek Enquirer and News*. The Civil Rights Movement was seen as a problem of the South, and Battle Creek was a long ways away from Alabama. The integration problems surfaced in big cities like Detroit, not Battle Creek. There were racial tensions, but like many small cities in the early 1960s, these were suppressed and not discussed.

Daisy received a telephone call at around 9:00 a.m. from her husband at Fales' Market. He made the call every day at around the same time to check on his wife. Daisy told Floyd that she was just getting ready to take a bath before going to meet with Audrey.

Daisy placed a call to the Battle Creek Health Center shortly thereafter, speaking with Irene Taylor. Daisy had a few questions regarding some paperwork related to her insurance. From what Irene could tell, Daisy seemed quite normal in her conversational tone.

At some point in the morning, she began to pack for work. A small brown paper sack was on the kitchen table, inside of which were a napkin and a banana. That morning Daisy prepared her lunch to be eaten on her afternoon break at the plant. A sandwich, a wedge of cheese and two pickles were each neatly wrapped in wax paper and laid out next to the open lunch sack. She had also put her white work shoes on the table in a paper bag to ensure she didn't forget them.

A few minutes later, just after 9:00 a.m., Daisy's phone rang again. This time it was the man with whom she'd been having an affair for the past two years, Raymond Mercer. She knew Ray from the plant, and their relationship was anything but a secret at Kellogg's. This wasn't the first time that Daisy had strayed from her husband. She had had other boyfriends over the years, and Raymond was simply the latest. He had called her simply to say, "Hello," and to say that he was looking forward to seeing her at the plant later that afternoon.

Around 9:30 a.m., Mae Tolls, a cleaning woman working at the Radford home on Juno Street, was working on the first floor of the home. She took a rug outside to shake it clean and noticed that Daisy's drapes were pulled open. It struck her as odd. Daisy usually didn't open her drapes until around 11:00 a.m., when she left. While Tolls had never spoken with Daisy, the two had waved to each other often, and she knew Daisy's weekday patterns. Thinking nothing else of it, she went about her work, doing some ironing in the basement laundry room.

Just before 10:00 a.m., Audrey Heminger called Daisy. Aside from the killer, Audrey was the last person to speak to Daisy before she died.

At some time after 10:00 a.m., Daisy's neighbor from across the street, Mrs. George DeFrance, saw someone standing at the breezeway at the Zick home at 100 Juno Street. The Zick home had a modest breezeway that was really just a simple covered space between the house and the garage. From what little Mrs. DeFrance could see, the person appeared to be a man, jumping up and down a little to battle the cold. He had dark hair, probably black from what she could tell. She could see that he was of medium height and was wearing a dark blue jacket, most likely of the Eisenhower-style variety. Daisy was known to have men over in the mornings when her husband was working and, in fact, had a reputation for having suitors to her home when her husband was away. So Mrs. DeFrance did not give the man a second thought. It never dawned on her how odd it was to see a man out in such cold weather without a car.

Approximately twenty minutes later, Mrs. DeFrance was letting her dog out and again glanced across the street at the Zick home. Daisy's side of the garage door was open. The Zick garage had two wooden doors. Daisy's was white with a large, distinctive metal Z on it, and Floyd's had a decorative picture of a man and woman riding a bicycle built for two. Mrs. DeFrance was struck by the fact that the door was left up and the car gone.

In such cold weather, people generally didn't leave their garage doors open, and Daisy never left hers open regardless of the weather. Missing from the garage was Daisy's car, a white 1959 Pontiac two-door model. It was a distinctive vehicle with fins that flanked the trunk on the rear. Mrs. DeFrance looked back over at the Zick home a few minutes later and noticed that curtains to the bedroom were still open. Daisy always opened her curtains by 11:00 a.m. every day, and she wouldn't have left the house without doing so. The fact that they were open earlier than usual struck Mrs. DeFrance as strange but not strange enough for her to investigate. Rather than check on her neighbor, Mrs. DeFrance retreated to the warmth of her home.

Audrey Heminger arrived at Vello's to have coffee with Daisy as planned, but her friend never showed. When Daisy didn't appear, Audrey was concerned but assumed that something had come up that had forced her friend to miss their meeting. When Audrey clocked in at the plant for the afternoon shift, there was no sign of Daisy, and according to her supervisor, she had not called in, which was unusual. Daisy was a creature of habit. She had not missed work before without calling in.

Audrey checked with Raymond Mercer to see if he knew why Daisy hadn't come into work. Raymond said that had spoken with her earlier in the morning, and as far as he knew, Daisy was planning to come into work as usual. On his break, he put on his coat to go out into the employee parking lot to see if Daisy's car was in her usual spot. There was no sign of her white Pontiac there.

Audrey called the Zick home, but there was no answer. Then she called Floyd at Fales' Market on Main Street around 12:30 p.m.

"I am worried about Daisy. She didn't meet me, and I wonder if she changed her plans? She usually calls if she does."

"No, Daisy planned on meeting you. She didn't show up?"

"No. And I checked over at the office and they haven't heard from her. She isn't at work yet. And she hasn't answered the phone. I'm kind of upset."

Floyd was worried as well. Daisy was a lot of things, but conscientious was near the top of the list.

"Something must be wrong. I'll go home right away and check."

Chances were that, with the stinging cold outside, his wife's car might have broken down. He gathered his coat and set out toward his home, heading east on Michigan Avenue.

At Evanston Road, across from the snow-blown third hole of the Pine Knoll Golf Course, he spotted Daisy's car on the other shoulder of the road. "It looked like our car," Floyd later recounted, "I slowed down, turned around, parked behind the car and looked at the license number. It was our car. I thought that Daisy had become sick. Maybe she was lying down inside the car.

"I got out and looked in the car. She wasn't in it. I got in the car to see if the motor would run. There were no keys in the ignition, but I used my set of keys to start it."

Perhaps it had temporarily broken down and Daisy had set off on foot? The car seemed just fine. Where was Daisy then? Floyd's concern began to rise. It would have been worse if he had seen the tiny smears of blood on the interior door near the handle. Floyd didn't look in the snow for footprints. If he had, he would have possibly seen a faint set of man's prints leading away from the car on the plowed shoulder.

Floyd got out of Daisy's car, got in his own and headed for his home. When he pulled up, he saw the garage door was open, and he became more concerned. Daisy had never left the door open before. With an attached garage, it would have simply made the house colder. But she was also worried about break-ins, so she always kept the house locked when she was home alone, despite the fact that they did not live in a crime-riddled area. After all, this was quiet Wattles Park, not downtown Battle Creek.

The door leading from the breezeway into the kitchen was unlocked and slightly ajar when Floyd reached it, another sign that something was wrong.

The Zick kitchen had an almost summer cottage feel, with knotted hardwood cabinet doors covered in a thick gloss of varnish. The oil furnace would have made the air dry on such a cold day, charged with static electricity. Seeing Daisy's lunch and shoes on the kitchen table was yet another ominous sign that something was amiss. If Daisy had broken down on the way to work, her lunch would have either been with her or at least in the Pontiac. The tan kitchen

The Zick garage left suspiciously open. *Courtesy of the Michigan State Police.*

rug was wadded up against the counter, as if someone had skidded on it. The linoleum in the kitchen was light, and he didn't notice signs of melted slush. Floyd called for Daisy but got no response besides the dull hum of the furnace in the basement.

Glancing into the living room, Floyd thought everything seemed ordinary. On the fireplace mantel were the twin photographs of him and his wife, mutely staring back at him. He did see a damp spot—melted slush—on the rug in the living room. Daisy never would have allowed something like that. She kept her home immaculate.

Moving into the bedroom, he didn't see his wife. What he saw was the chenille, white flower–patterned spread slightly disheveled on the bed, yet another indication that something was wrong. Daisy never would have left the bed in such disarray. The more dismaying sight, however, was that the bedspread was soaked in several spots with something dark red—blood. It looked as if the blood had been drizzled on the bed, with the largest spot measuring about two inches across. At the foot of the bed Daisy's purse sat upright with the contents thrown about as if it had been dumped out and

The Zicks' master bedroom with Daisy's purse. *Courtesy of the Michigan State Police.*

then dropped. Her green wallet and matching checkbook were tossed on the bedspread. Floyd's worries escalated as he processed each new piece of information. Daisy would never have left the house without her purse, and the blood, if that's what it was, was not a positive sign.

But where was his wife?

He dashed back through the kitchen and noticed something else out of place. The Zicks had a small opening in the wall between the living room and the southwest corner of the kitchen that was ornamented with a polished wooden ledge. On that ledge was a small plant in a ceramic shoe and the connection box for the phone. Floyd noticed that the wire that connected the tan cradle of the telephone to the wall box was cut. The phone sat on a small desk in the kitchen. Floyd moved down the hall and passed the bathroom, where nothing seemed at all out of the ordinary. He turned his attention to the spare bedroom that he and Daisy used mostly for entertaining purposes. It was the last room in the small ranch house that for him to check.

In the corner, he noticed the hi-fi console had been pushed out from the wall. Droplets of dark maroon blood splattered the walls and the varnished woodwork on the closet doorframe, where he saw his first glimpse of his wife. He saw her feet first, sticking out from behind the bed in her black and gold slippers, and a hint of her brown slacks. One leg was twisted unnaturally. Floyd crept forward cautiously, worried about what he might find.

Daisy, as Floyd Zick and investigators found her in the spare bedroom. *Courtesy of the Michigan State Police.*

Daisy lay on the floor between the bed and the wall. It was hard to distinguish her features from the blood that soaked her body. Her hands were behind her back, and her chest was crimson with her own congealed blood. The carpet had several pools of dark blood, testimony to the savage injuries she had suffered. Floyd lowered himself next to his wife. He mumbled her name, "Daisy…Daisy…," but she didn't respond. When he reached out and touched her, he confirmed what he suspected—she was dead. The amount of blood caused him to assume that she had been shot. The house was so small that he knew the killer was no longer there. Whoever had done this had taken her car and fled. For Floyd Zick, being in that room had to give him a most eerie sense of loneliness—in the house with his wife's body and all that blood with the quiet of the Michigan winter storm outside.

Because the phone upstairs was cut, Floyd ran downstairs to the basement, where they had a second telephone in a makeshift recreation room. He called Fales' Market and spoke to his boss, the assistant manager Lowell MacDonald. Floyd told him that his wife had been shot and asked MacDonald to contact the police. At 1:15 p.m., MacDonald placed the call to the Michigan State Police Post Forty-six in Battle Creek, reporting a murder at 100 Juno Street in Wattles Park. MacDonald had called it in as a shooting based on what Floyd had told him.

Floyd then made a call to Audrey Heminger to tell her that Daisy was dead. The word would spread through Kellogg's in a matter of an hour, even before an announcement on the local radio station. For fifteen long lonely minutes, Floyd Zick remained in his house alone with his beloved dead Daisy.

Chapter 2

TO THE BITTER END

Returning to the kitchen, he [Floyd Zick] *noticed the telephone wire had been cut. "I ran into the spare bedroom. The first thing I notice was that the hi-fi was out of place. Then I saw her lying on the floor." He went to his wife's side and saw that she was dead.*

Battle Creek Enquirer and News
January 14, 1963

There is a tendency to look at any old police investigation and point out the flaws. Since the Daisy Zick murder remains unsolved, it is easy to look back with twenty-twenty hindsight and say, "They should have looked into this," or "I can't believe they did that." Armchair quarterbacking of murders is easy and dangerously seductive to undertake. The truth is that none of us were there. In 1963, the scientific investigation of a crime was still in its infancy compared to today. And the officers handled the case as they did, as per the rules and procedures of the day.

The call to the state police that triggered their response was not broadcast to the officers that were already dispatched. Instead, it was called in via the telephone. At the time, there was a rift of sorts between the state police in Battle Creek and the local authorities. Also, technology was catching up with police communications, allowing people with the right gear to eavesdrop on radio calls. As Trooper Ralph Kartheu put it, "There were a few people out there listening to our radio calls. We didn't want the press showing up, and we didn't want the other agencies to just rush in." Ralph himself got the call

The Zick home after investigators arrived. *Courtesy of the Michigan State Police.*

while at lunch at a local restaurant. In the age before cellphones and walkie-talkies on every trooper, procedure was to radio in where you were eating, and if dispatch needed you, it simply called the restaurant.

On his way to the Zick home, Kartheu passed Daisy's white Pontiac Bonneville. Just prior to lunch, Ralph had pulled over near the car to execute a car investigation (CI). He checked the vehicle over, finding it unlocked and without the keys. He had no idea that the abandoned Pontiac had any links to the crime scene he was approaching.

Michigan State Police detective Charles Conn and troopers Robert Dockery and Ralph Kartheu were the first on the scene at 100 Juno Street. Floyd Zick was pulled aside and questioned about what he had seen and touched in the house. Kartheu made sure the home was secure while waiting for additional investigators.

Tiny Juno Street became a hub of activity with all the police cars centered on the Zick home. The state police troopers were soon joined by officers from the county's small sheriff's office. They sized up the one-story brick ranch in cold analytical descriptions. It was a small working-class-family home: living room, kitchen, two bedrooms and a bathroom. Its appearance was indiscrete, except that, now, physical evidence of a murder was scattered almost everywhere.

Detective Charles "Charlie" Conn was a seasoned investigator. He had a low, gentle voice and was known for being tenacious in his investigating style. At the same time, Detective Conn was not one of those officers who was immersed in his work. It was a job that he did, just like someone working in a factory. His white-gray hair was worn short, and his long face did not belay the complexities of the tasks that lay before him that afternoon. Detective Conn was a man with a difficult past. He had been born in the rural community of Branch County, Michigan, on January 16, 1914. His mother had died when he was young, and his brothers and sister had been parsed out to aunts and uncles to raise. In Charlie's case, this meant a childhood with one of his aunts and uncles in nearby Colon. Charlie worked a number of jobs during the early years of the Great Depression, including a stint in the Civilian Conservation Corps (CCC) and a year of business school. His stepfather had been a foreman on a road construction crew and employed his son in the backbreaking labor in his youth.

If he had his way, he would have been a conservation officer—it was his first job choice. Instead, Charlie joined the state police on a fluke. He and a friend took the test to become troopers, but his friend failed where Charlie

Charles Conn of the Michigan State Police. This investigation would consume several years of his career. *Courtesy Mary McMillen.*

passed. Like many troopers in the 1930s and '40s, his life was one of being moved from post to post, expanding his skills and experience. He had been assigned to East Lansing, Traverse City, and in 1945, he had been posted in the Michigan thumb area operating out of the Bad Axe post. Charlie and two other troopers were the entire Michigan State Police presence for the thumb region during the duration of the war. It was in Bad Axe that he met and married his wife, Margaret. They had two children, a daughter who died young and a son, also named Charlie.

Detective Conn was a quiet, serious man. According to his son, he was a stickler for details and the rule of law. Fellow officers noted that Charlie didn't take notes on pads of paper but scribbled on anything he had—the back of match packets, napkins, receipts or anything else he had in his possession. His hair had gone white early in life. He wanted to spend his time off with his family, which, given his childhood, was easy to understand. He had been an avid golfer since his youth, and when he could, he squeezed in hunting and fishing as well. The Zick case was one that would prove to be one of his most difficult and challenging. Little did he realize that he was really just one of the first generation of investigators that would tackle the murder.

A quick check of the scene told Detective Conn that the Michigan State Police crime lab needed to be involved. This was the kind of crime that was beyond the capabilities of a local state police post. A Detective Sergeant Christensen and Detective Olney led a team of two other investigators—Donald Hannah and William Slowinski—to Battle Creek from Lansing. They arrived at around 4:00 p.m., leaving the troopers that initially arrived at the scene to attempt to ascertain exactly what had happened.

Floyd Zick was still at home, somewhat dazed but letting the officers in. The troopers told him not to touch anything. They began to pepper him with questions as they fanned out in the tiny house, looking for the obvious clues before the arrival of the crime lab boys.

One of the first men on the scene from the Calhoun County Sheriff's Department was Undersheriff Wayne R. Fitch. The sheriff's office usually deferred to the state police on murder cases, but it was common for the sheriff's office to put one of its officers on the case as well. Where state police tended to be rotated in and out of cities, sheriff's office employees were local and often provided necessary inside information.

Outwardly, Fitch wore horn-rimmed glasses and appeared to be more of a schoolteacher than a sheriff. He had been orphaned and adopted as a child and did not know who his birth parents were. Fitch was forty-three years old and had been a member of the sheriff's department since 1944. He was born in 1919 in Ann Arbor, Michigan, where he met his wife, Wilma. When he joined the department, he began as a radio dispatcher and turnkey. In 1956, Sheriff Jess Purcell promoted him to chief deputy, and a year later, he was made captain. Two years later, he was appointed to the role of undersheriff and made the chief investigator for the department. In this role, the more complex cases that required in-depth investigation fell on Fitch's shoulders.

When you talk to people who knew Wayne Fitch, they tell you that he had a stern "cop voice" that immediately demanded respect and response. Fitch also had a "watch-eye," an eye that was unfocused. In casual conversations with him, you'd never notice it. When he stared you down, however, the watch-eye gave an air of fearsome authority to his persona.

He was detail oriented and always tried to cover every alternative. One year, when he had been assigned to work at the Calhoun County Fair, there had been a harness-racing accident on the track. The deputies cut the horses free, which caused a stir because the owners were upset over the damage done to their tack. Rather than let his men look foolish again, Fitch meticulously planned for each officer's role in the event of a similar accident. One of the deputies was specifically tasked with removing (not cutting) the harnesses off the horses to which the deputy responded, "Hell, I can't even take off my wife's bra!" But Fitch didn't care. Detailed planning was the key to his personality.

Wayne Fitch was not only an employee in the sheriff's department, but he was also a fixture in the community. He was vice-president of the Fraternal Order of Police Lodge 121, a member of the Calhoun County Safety Commission (where he chaired the "Safety Sunday" committee) and a member of the Battle Creek Metropolitan Club. He was a member of the Southern Michigan Law Enforcement Association and the Michigan Sheriff's Association.

Fitch was an elder in the First Presbyterian Church in Marshall, where he was also a Sunday School teacher and a member of the Men's Council. His involvement in the community also included the Masons and the St. Alban's Lodge. The church was an important part of his life and gave him a wide range of connections in the county. His sense of community and his dogged attention to details made Fitch the sheriff's department's go-to man on the crime scene, even though the state police would take the lead role.

The spare bedroom where Daisy's body had been found had one window that was locked and covered with venetian blinds and drapes, both of which were closed. The RCA console hi-fi in the room was normally on the south wall but had been jerked to where her body had come to rest. She was lying on the power cord still plugged into the wall. The bed with its bookcase headboard apparently had not been moved, but a small, framed photograph on the dresser on the north wall had been knocked over as Daisy had struggled in the last moments of her life.

The light carpet in the spare bedroom had bloodstains on it. Most were light, but at least two were small pools. The south and east wall of the room were also spattered with Daisy's

The spare bedroom with the small photo knocked over and the RCA console hi-fi. *Courtesy of the Michigan State Police.*

blood. The stains on the south wall were smudged, as if someone had brushed against them in a sweeping-arched motion. To the investigators, it seemed that Daisy might have been sitting on the floor against the south wall at one point before sliding westward to her final position on the floor. The pattern of spatter on the wall indicated that many of her wounds were inflicted while she was on the floor of the spare bedroom. The colorful striped bedspread in the room revealed more spatter drops and at least one spot with a bloody smear. Despite the obvious struggle that had taken place in the room, five neatly stacked 78 RPM records were on the bedspread, undisturbed. Where Floyd had thought his wife had been shot, Detective Conn knew differently. These were the patterns of a stabbing.

Daisy was wearing a buttoned-up white blouse—soaked, by the time authorities arrived, in the dull maroon of her blood—and brown wool slacks. The pants were unzipped and pulled below her waist by about six inches. Her black and gold house slippers seemed oddly out of place with the violence she had suffered. Her white panties were still in place as was her blood soaked bra. At first glimpse, at least, it didn't appear that she had been sexually assaulted. That would be something that the medical examiner would have to confirm.

Daisy, lying against the wall on the floor. The blood smears indicate she slid from a sitting position to this final position. *Courtesy of the Michigan State Police.*

Daisy's head was pointed to the southwest, and her mouth was in contact with the leg of the bed. She was lying on her back with her hands tied behind her, bound tightly with the sash from her housecoat. Her left foot pointed to the northeast, and her right leg was bent at the knee with the foot pointing to the southeast.

Closer examination indicated that she had been stabbed repeatedly, mostly in the left breast and in the left back. Her lipstick was smeared on her upper lip, and a bit was on the right sleeve of her blouse. A greasy smudge was also on the right sleeve of her blood-soaked blouse. Another dirty smudge appeared on her panties in the left pelvic area.

The team went to the master bedroom located in the southwest section of the house at the west end of the hallway. It was the larger of the two rooms, though it was only nine and a half feet square. An inexpensive light fixture in the center of the ceiling was the room's chief source of light in the evenings. When investigators entered, the drapes were partially drawn in the room. There was a double bed, nightstand, chest of drawers and dressing table and chair. On the

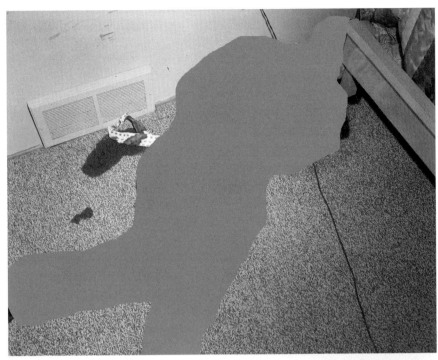

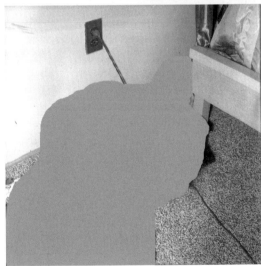

Above: This image shows the tie from her robe that was tied behind her back. *Courtesy of the Michigan State Police.*

Right: This perspective shows Daisy's resting place on the power cord near the edge of the bed. *Courtesy of the Michigan State Police.*

floor of the bedroom was a flimsy blue and red dressing robe. The lightweight garment resembled a nightgown more than a robe. It lay on the floor where it had apparently been discarded, covered a little bit by the bedspread. This was the source of the matching sash that tied Daisy's hands behind her back.

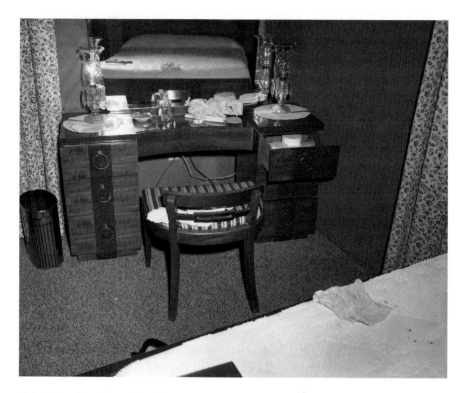

Daisy's dressing table as found by the investigators. *Courtesy of the Michigan State Police.*

The chenille bedspread was white with a pattern stitched into it. It was disturbed with the faint outline of a person, as if Daisy had been thrown onto it. The white spread was also splotched with her drying blood and a lighter crimson smear in one spot, which turned out to be her lipstick. Whoever had tied Daisy up must have turned her over on the bed to tie her hands, causing her face to leave a trace of lipstick.

Daisy's green wallet and checkbook were near the foot of the bed and looked as though they had been dropped there hurriedly. The light brown purse was on the carpeted floor at the foot of the bed and was upright. There was no sign that the drawers had been opened or searched, an indication that robbery was not the primary motive for the crime. Besides, few robberies ever resulted in the kind of brutality that the police had seen so far in the crime scene.

A check of the bathroom yielded nothing out of the ordinary. Whatever the chaos was in Daisy's last few minutes of life, it apparently had not taken place there.

The kitchen, however, was not in order. The telephone on the small ledge had its wires cut near the box that connected it to the wall. The investigators removed the cut wires in the hopes of being able to match the cuts to some sort of weapon.

The bunched-up carpet at the sink indicated that someone had run and possibly slid on the carpet on the smooth kitchen floor. It was becoming apparent that whatever had occurred in the Zick home had not been confined to the room where Daisy's body had been found. There had been a struggle throughout the tiny brick ranch.

The front door was unlocked too, which, from what Floyd told the investigators, was out of character for his wife. The side entryway was often left unlocked, according to Floyd, but the door leading into the house was kept secured. A check of the doormat near the front door found it dry. If someone came in through this door, he didn't leave any melted snow or slush. There was no sign of the door having been forced open either.

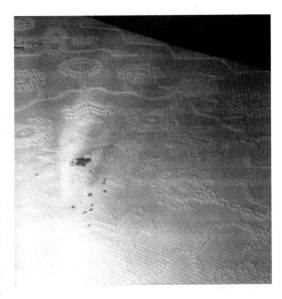

The bedspread in the master bedroom with the telltale sign of blood, indicating some of her injuries took place here or prior to being here. *Courtesy of the Michigan State Police.*

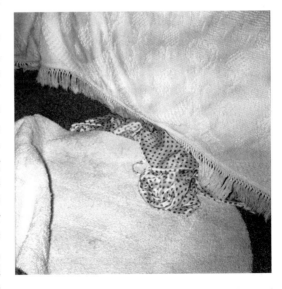

On the floor next to the bed was the sash of the robe that was used to tie up Daisy. *Courtesy of the Michigan State Police.*

The door that led to the breezeway from the kitchen. *Courtesy of the Michigan State Police.*

The kitchen wastebasket was empty of trash. Richard Stevens of the prosecutor's office noted that Daisy had been a meticulously tidy person. There was a paper bag in the wastebasket that acted as a trash bag, and she had taken the time to cut out a small piece of cardboard and place it in the bottom so that the bag didn't tear under the weight of the garbage. It gave them a clue as to how meticulous Daisy was in keeping her house clean.

There were a few dirty dishes in the kitchen sink. The police focused on the small wooden-handled knife found there. It was not a kitchen knife but a wooden-handled Spoilage knife, a type of short-bladed box cutter, similar to those used in the Kellogg's Factory. The crime lab team secured it for consideration as the murder weapon. There was a small dot of darkness on the blade. To the troopers' trained eyes, it appeared to be blood. Had someone stabbed Daisy and then taken the time to wash off the murder weapon before leaving it behind?

The door leading to the breezeway and the garage was unlocked, as Floyd Zick had found it. A check was made of all the windows, which proved they were hooked shut. The dry mat at the front door pointed to the breezeway as the route of entrance.

The garage revealed very little. The door that connected the garage to the kitchen did, however, offer a clue to the violence. There was a smear of blood on the knob of the garage side of the door. Whoever had left the Zick home had to have Daisy's blood on him and had left the mark while closing the garage door.

As Detectives Conn and Trooper Kartheu looked over the house, they noted that it was exceptionally clean and orderly, a stark contrast to the violence that had erupted inside.

The boys from the state police crime lab had a grueling task ahead of them. The entire house had to be checked for physical evidence and prints. Testing for blood had to be done in several rooms. Sergeant Dan Myre and a trooper named Hein took over this portion of the difficult task. The cramped house made it difficult for the various officers to move around each other. Normally, the officers would have moved outside to give the men from the crime lab room to work, but the stinging cold outside ruled that out. When the *Battle Creek Enquirer and News* learned of the murder, its photographer was allowed into the house, putting the evidence at additional risk of tampering.

As they moved around the home, the lab workers' attempts to pick up fingerprints was stymied. From what the technicians could tell, Daisy had used some sort of polish or oil on the surfaces of the furniture throughout the house. The substance obscured any usable latent fingerprints they hoped to lift. Despite this, they recovered twelve prints that somehow had managed to endure. These would have to be maintained and tested against everyone who had been in the house to see if any not eliminated potentially belonged to the killer.

Trooper Bob "Doc" Dockery made the mistake of leaving his fingerprints at the crime scene. This wasn't the first time he had made this mistake. He had done it a year or so earlier, when a young man had been killed working at a gas station on I-94. After the print was identified at the state police crime lab in Lansing the next day, Detective Dan Meirs of the crime lab told "Doc" that if he left his prints at a murder scene again, he would break his arm.

After checking for fingerprints, the crime lab employees turned their attention to the Spoilage knife found in the sink. It sat in a rubber-coated wire basket, as if it had been tossed there to be washed later. Overall the knife was seven and one-half inches in length with a three-and-one-half-inch blade. It had a wooden handle, and the blade itself was flat at the front, rather than pointed, with a long sharp edge and a tiny sharp point. Most of the officers from the Battle Creek post recognized it as a factory box cutter, similar to those used at Kellogg's where Daisy worked. Initially, it may not seem that such a knife would be used in the kitchen in food preparation, but these knives were commonplace and easily taken from the plant. Employees often used them at home as paring knives or for woodworking. Was this the murder weapon? If so, why would the killer have left it for police to find?

There was a small spot on the blunt edge of the blade. The spot tested positive for blood. Floyd explained that the knife was indeed owned by the Zicks. Daisy had used it the night before to cut a chicken for dinner. Daisy usually cleaned her utensils after use, but she either hadn't gotten to this knife the night before or it was something other than chicken blood on the blade. The knife was carefully removed for further examination back at the laboratory in Lansing. The sink was also tested for blood, and the initial results showed faint traces. Did the killer wash off the murder weapon in the sink before leaving or was it residue from the night before? There was not enough blood to test to see if it was from a human or an animal.

Back in the bedroom, Daisy's purse and wallet were scrutinized for any possible clues. It seemed inconceivable that this was merely a robbery gone wrong, though the fact that the contents of the purse had been dumped out originally pointed to theft as a possible motive. The purse revealed no fingerprints or any sign of blood. What investigators found was two folded one-dollar bills, a quarter, three nickels and two pennies. A Ronson Adonis lighter with the initials D.M.Z., a Sheaffer ballpoint pen and a rat-tail comb were also discovered. The Zicks' checkbook did not reveal much either. Their balance was listed as $18.99. There were seventeen blank checks remaining, none unaccounted for. In her purse, her paycheck from Kellogg's for $25.96 after taxes was found. Floyd Zick told the investigators that Daisy had $45.00 in her purse the last he knew, though now that money apparently was gone. The lab team packaged the wallet away to check it for prints. It was possible that the killer had dumped it out and had left his or her prints on it accidently.

A small white button was found on the floor of the master bedroom that seemed out of place. The Zick home, aside from the murder scene, was immaculate. Yet here was a button on the floor in plain sight—something that Daisy surely would have picked up. More importantly, the button did not match any of the clothing that she was wearing. Was this a button that had been torn off during the struggle in the last moments of her life? The button was retained as possible evidence.

Checking near the body, the officers spotted something in the cold air return near where Daisy lay. Removing the object, they found a single black wingtip shoe. It didn't match any of the shoes in the house. It was a bizarre find that seemed to have nothing to do with the crime scene.

The search for fibers and hairs began late in the afternoon and was, at best, a long and tedious process. Led by Donald Hannah, five troopers from the crime lab began the delicate and time-consuming task. They started with the victim herself. Checking Daisy's body was a difficult procedure given the amount of time that had passed from her death and the amount of blood present. From behind her right ear, the investigators removed a small yellow cotton fiber. It was placed in a glass tube for future analysis.

Other yellow cotton fibers were recovered. One was lifted from the bloodstained bedspread, which had been adhered there by the drying blood of the victim. Even at a cursory glance, it appeared to be the same sort of cotton fiber as recovered from behind Daisy's ear. Other fibers were recovered in the house as well, but the yellow ones stood out since one was found on Daisy's body. Even to an untrained eye, these appeared to come from yellow cotton hunting or work gloves common to the time.

Samples of hair were recovered from the carpet and furniture as well. All of these were saved for future analysis. Two samples were taken from Daisy, from her head and pubic area. Floyd Zick was asked to provide the same samples for comparison.

Daisy's blouse was examined carefully. In addition to being soaked in blood, it also had a small smudge of dirt or grease, a smear of medium red lipstick and spots of facial makeup. Numerous holes in the back and over the left breast came from the puncture wounds that had killed Daisy.

Daisy's brown wool slacks revealed more. The zipper was pulled most of the way down but was bunched up with fabric. It appeared that someone had tried to pull it open so hard that it had jammed. The investigators could only speculate whether this was done by Daisy or her assailant and whether it prevented her attack from being a sexual assault as well. From her slacks, several small yellow fibers were recovered and carefully preserved.

Her bra, or what was left of it, was checked as well. The white bra was dark maroon from her blood. Eight punctures riddled the fabric, testimony to the violence unleashed on her. Her murderer had stabbed at her breasts, perhaps an indication of the nature of her killer.

From the master bedroom, several red flakes were discovered on the floor that drew the attention of Hannah's investigating team. Closer observation showed that they were nails with polish on them. Daisy's body was checked again, and she was found to have chipped nails on her right ring and middle finger. They checked under her fingernails for signs of skin but found none. The fact that the fingernails were found in the master bedroom seemed to confirm the investigators' theory that a struggle took place there, in which Daisy broke two of her fingernails trying to fend off her attacker.

The team shifted to the garage since the killer had taken her car after her murder. Little was found except on the east garage door. On the outside door, a yellow fiber was discovered three-quarters of an inch above the knob.

Finding that fiber helped advance the investigators in trying to piece together what happened to Daisy. From the position of the fibers outside and inside, it was possible to surmise that these bright yellow fibers came from gloves worn by the killer. Such gloves were commonly worn by hunters and fishermen. They were also worn by some of the workers at Kellogg's and Post Cereals for work in the factory. For now, it was simply a theory, but one that warranted further checking.

By law, Daisy's body could not be removed until the Calhoun County Medical Examiner ruled her as dead. While it seemed like a formality, it was strictly adhered to. In 1963, the role of medical examiner was a part-time job, and it took several hours for Dr. Richard Bloch to finally arrive at the Zick home. In the 1960s, Calhoun County experienced roughly one murder a year. Most of these were second-degree murders, or crimes of passion. They were quick, vicious affairs but not on the scale of what had unfolded in the tiny Zick home. There was little that could have prepared Dr. Bloch for the brutality of the death that he was about to witness on Juno Street.

His examination only took seconds, and at 4:40 p.m., he ruled that Daisy was indeed dead. By then, rigor mortis had begun to set in, enhanced by the heat in the tiny home. Based on his observations, Bloch placed the time of death at around 11:00 a.m. The Farley Funeral Home of Battle Creek was contacted to come and take Daisy's body away. Her autopsy was to be done at the funeral home that evening. It would be years before the local county hospitals were equipped to handle such cases.

After a long day of checking, the Zick home had not yielded much in the way of evidence for the investigators. Inspector Charles Cobb faced the next daunting task of checking Daisy's car for evidence, followed by digging into her personal life. One thing was becoming clear, however: someone had come to 100 Juno Street with the single purpose of killing Daisy Zick.

Daisy's autopsy at the Farley Funeral Home was performed by Dr. William Walters under the eyes of two of the investigators of the case. Like Dr. Bloch, Dr. Walters's role as a medical examiner was a part-time job and rarely for a case as complicated as this one. Nevertheless, her clothes were carefully removed and turned over to the detectives, who kept them as evidence. It was clear that Daisy's killer had resorted to unnecessary measures.

Trooper Ralph Kartheu was present, along with a stenographer, at the autopsy. By Kartheu's account, it started out badly. Dr. Walters stated, "We are beginning the autopsy of a forty-three-year-old male—" before Kartheu cut him off, telling him that he was incorrect.

"Trooper, who are you to tell me anything about how to do an autopsy?"

"This is a female victim, doctor."

"That doesn't matter," Walters replied.

"It does if we go to court. They can call into question the validity of your findings." Walters begrudgingly corrected his error and continued.

She had fifteen puncture wounds surrounding her left breast. Eight of the wounds there were clustered closely together. There was a laceration on her left collarbone. Four slashing cuts were found on her upper left arm. Six additional puncture wounds were on the left side of her back, just to the right of her left armpit. The investigators felt that the wounds on her back had most likely been inflicted either when the killer had tied up her hands while she was facedown on the bed or when she had potentially tried to flee her assailant.

The slashing wounds on her arms showed that she attempted to fend off her attacker by blocking his stabs. Either the stabs or her resistance had led to the fracture of three of her ribs. For the detectives, these wounds revealed that Daisy did not go down without a fight. She had struggled with her assailant until he had been forced to tie her hands.

There was other damage she had endured. Her body showed signs of bruising behind her right ear. The blow there had been sufficient to cause hemorrhaging. It would have been strong enough to leave Daisy dazed, perhaps for a few minutes. The bruising indicated that she had been alive when the blow had been delivered, and it was perhaps from an early part of the struggle that took place at 100 Juno Street.

Detective Sergeant Dan Myre had brought the Spoilage knife that had been recovered in her kitchen. Dr. Walters looked at the blade and claimed that in his opinion, the blade had not been used to kill Daisy. The stubby blunt end of the blade did not seem to match the wounds that she received, which was why he initially justified ruling it out as the weapon used to kill her. At the same time, Dr. Walters did not offer any other description about the kind of knife that would have been used if it not the Spoilage knife.

Detective Conn and others on the investigative team remained unconvinced. While a direct thrusting of the blade could not duplicate the stab wounds that Daisy had, a thrust angled downward would have allowed its tiny point to duplicate the wounds. Given the sharp edge of the blade, it could easily have caused the injuries. Despite the medical examiner's contrary finding, the investigators were sure they had the murder weapon and tagged it into evidence.

Daisy's official cause of death was exsanguination—the scientific term for bleeding to death.

———•◦•———

That afternoon, almost as an afterthought, the investigators called the Calhoun County prosecutor's office. County prosecuting attorney Noble Moore was furious. A vicious murder had taken place in his county, and he was hearing about it only *after* the investigation was underway? This wasn't the first time either. There had been a bank robbery in Teknosha, Michigan, and the state police post commander in Battle Creek, Joe Svoke, had failed to bring him in right away. To the rigid Moore, it was another deliberate slight on the part of the state police to disrespect his office. In his mind, the first thing they should have done was reach out to him.

Noble Moore was a World War II combat veteran and highly respected in the community. He was a brigadier general in the Michigan National Guard, and when he spoke, he had a booming, commanding voice that could shake a room. Even those that worked for him referred to him as "General Moore." At the time of the crime, he had been working at the National Guard in Detroit and could not have been contacted anyway, but that detail didn't seem to matter to the attorney. Moore sent some of the junior attorneys from his office to the scene immediately, while he arrived later in the day.

There was a reason for his bravado and bluster—Moore got results. During his seven years as prosecutor, he had overseen twenty-five murder trials, almost all with convictions.

Murders in Calhoun County were rare to begin with, and there was no formal protocol in cases such as Daisy Zick's. Still, Moore was angered by this perceived slight, an attitude that would plague the case in the following days.

———•◦•———

Detective Conn, Undersheriff Wayne Fitch and their investigators began to try piecing together what had happened at 100 Juno Street earlier that day. The investigators wanted to see if they could reassemble Daisy's death in the hope that it might offer them some insight as to who had killed her.

The team surmised that Daisy was probably preparing to go meet her friend Audrey on the morning of her murder. Based on the smears of makeup on her blouse, they assumed she was most likely putting it on when she was drawn to the breezeway and found someone at the door.

The view of the Zick home from the DeFrance home on the day of the murder. *Courtesy of the Michigan State Police.*

An interview with neighbor Mrs. DeFrance seemed to point to a time and entry point for the murderer. The person at the walkway door was either someone who Daisy knew or who had tricked her into allowing him entry. From her bedroom, where she was likely getting dressed, there was a window that would have allowed her to see anyone at the exterior door. If the person had let himself in, she wouldn't have been able to see her murderer since the door from the kitchen to the breezeway was solid and the Zicks kept this door locked. Daisy would have had to open the door for whoever was there, perhaps a hint that she knew who it was.

From the disarray of the rug, the investigators gathered there was some sort of confrontation in the kitchen. Daisy must have made a dash for the telephone at some point, probably to call for help. On a rotary phone before the era of 911, it was folly on her part. Even worse, she had turned her back to her murderer.

The attacker was most likely right-handed and struck her from behind, hitting her behind her right ear. Yet at the same time, the stabs to the back seemed to indicate a left-handed assailant. The blow was brutal and hard. Daisy was stunned and probably fled for the master bedroom. The thinking of the officers the day of the crime was that her killer first cut the telephone cord and then pursued her.

Daisy had either collapsed onto the bed facedown or been forced there by her killer. Either way, the imprint of her body on the bedspread seemed to

The severed phone line in the kitchen. *Courtesy of the Michigan State Police.*

support that she had been on the bed at some point. The broken fingernails in the bedroom indicated some sort of struggle there. At some point, the killer must have overpowered tiny Daisy because he would have had to open her closet to pull out her robe. For him to do this, Daisy must have been stunned or semiconscious, otherwise she would have taken the opportunity to flee. Tossing the robe aside, the murderer used the sash to tie Daisy's arms behind her.

With the victim subdued, the killer could now complete the job he had come to do. The killer first struck at her from behind, slashing at her with the knife and leaving spots of her blood in the bedroom. The areas where she was hit supported the theory of a right-handed assailant.

Daisy was tough though. Despite her injuries, she was able to break free and run, or more likely stagger, away, her arms tied behind her back. When she reached the guest bedroom, she tried to seek cover behind the hi-fi near the wall.

Her murderer would then have pulled the hi-fi out of the way to begin slashing at her, spattering the room and its occupants with blood. The vast majority of her wounds took place there, on the floor of the spare bedroom, as her killer savagely tore into her with the knife. Daisy died, slumping down, smearing blood on the wall as she collapsed. Her death would have been obvious, but whoever had killed her had kept stabbing and slashing at Daisy. It was pure overkill and indicated to most who investigated the crime that the killer was in a complete rage.

The murderer then straddled her body and, in a frenzy, stabbed at her chest.

If the Spoilage knife was the murder weapon as the police believed, the killer must have washed it off before inexplicably leaving it behind. He must have gotten into Daisy's purse prior to leaving to steal her forty-five dollars and the keys to her car. It was a paltry amount of money for the brutality involved in the crime.

Whoever the perpetrator was had put in considerable time planning to kill Daisy. He had not driven to the home that day but, instead, must have either walked there in the drifting snow and stinging winter wind or been dropped off by someone else, a potential alternative. The walk would have made the killer's thighs sting from the cold wind and feet ache from the crunching of the snow; the blowing snowfall would have stung at his face. It was a walk that would have taken considerable determination and purpose. Furthermore, Daisy did not work the typical nine-to-five day; she worked the afternoon shift. Her murderer must have known her routine to show up while she was still at home. The investigators felt that the brutality of the attack indicated that whoever it was had a grudge against her, one that spawned such a savage stabbing. Only the anger that drove them to murder would have propelled them onward.

Some officers offered alternate theories at this stage of the investigation. The theory that the killer had an accomplice who dropped him off at the Zick home is one that also happened to fit the physical evidence available, but, unfortunately, the idea did not get them any closer to locating the killer.

Gathering evidence quickly from a murder was important, and the Zick home was not the only source of physical clues. A team was sent to look over the 1959 white Pontiac Bonneville coupe. The hard-top car was still on Michigan Avenue, snow drifting around the wheels. A careful sweep was made of the vehicle. The investigators even noticed the mileage: 35,517, the last mile of which the killer had driven. The car was towed to the garage of the Battle Creek State Police Post, where it could be evaluated in a more careful manner.

The investigators broadened their inquiries from the Juno Street neighborhood to the people that Daisy was supposed to interact with that day. Audrey Heminger, Daisy's coffee companion, was met at Kellogg's by a police officer and taken to the Battle Creek State Police Post to give a statement. She had little to offer other than that Daisy had not showed up for their coffee date and she had reached out to Floyd. Audrey did not know anyone that wanted to harm her friend. Despite Audrey's cooperation, Noble Moore was aggressive in his questioning of her, his tone downright abrasive.

The rumors of Daisy's affairs seemed to feed the prosecutor's probing. Audrey did tell investigators that Daisy was having an affair with Raymond Mercer at Kellogg's but that she did not know more details. The prosecutor seemed to feel that she knew more than she was telling the officers. He made a note that she needed to be brought in again for further questioning.

All eyes initially turned to Daisy's husband. Throughout the day, Floyd Zick had remained at his home as the investigators performed their delicate work. Detective Conn questioned him during that time. Did Daisy have any enemies? No, none that Floyd could think of. Daisy had been married before, but there didn't seem to be any problems with her former husband. Her son from the previous marriage, James King, was out of town in New York, visiting his aunt. The police assured Floyd that James would be contacted by the end of the day to confirm where he was and let him know what had happened to his mother. When he heard the news, James immediately began the trip back to Battle Creek.

An investigator's first instinct when faced with such a violent crime is to focus on the people closest to the victim and either rule them out or find evidence that implicates them. Detective Conn asked Floyd if he would be willing to submit to a polygraph test, if to do nothing more than to clear his name. Floyd agreed. There was nothing in his demeanor that pointed to him as the killer, but he was still considered a suspect.

Investigators held out hope that the Pontiac Bonneville could offer some clues or, better yet, that a witness had seen someone walking away from the car. On such a cold day, a person walking along the busiest road in this part of the county would have been something to take note of.

Chapter 3

THE MYSTERIOUS MAN ON
MICHIGAN AVENUE

A theory that more than one person may have been involved in the slaying of Mrs. Daisy Zick gained support last night with an account from a motorist who may have seen the killer drive away with a second man.

Battle Creek Enquirer and News
January 15, 1963

The state police combed the Zicks' Pontiac Bonneville for any potential evidence that it might yield. Daisy's car was remarkably clean, just like her house, which made some of the evidence easy to spot. There were blood smears on the white exterior of the passenger-side door in the area near the end of the door handle, similar to what would be left if someone with blood on his arm had brushed up against the car.

As they worked their way around and inside the 3,895 pounds of tough Detroit steel, the police searched for anything else of value and lifted over a half dozen fingerprints. On the chrome strip just under the front of the hood, about twenty-two inches to the left of the right side (facing the front of the vehicle), they discovered a faint fabric impression. It was the kind of mark that would have been made if someone had leaned onto the front of the car. There was no way to tell if the spot was made by the killer, a mechanic working on the car or a fellow shopper bumping into the vehicle in a parking lot. A negative photo impression was made of the imprint, nevertheless.

A closer inspection of the front of the car revealed several yellow fibers caught on the bottom of the front bumper by the hood release lever. These

Daisy's Pontiac Bonneville. Note the smear of blood from someone brushing against the passenger door. *Courtesy of the Michigan State Police.*

were carefully removed and saved to compare against those found in the Zick home.

Any car picks up a lot of fingerprints, and Daisy's was no exception. Most were fragments that would take weeks to exclude by getting prints from service station attendants and anyone that remembered riding in the car. Initially, there were three that stood out as the best samples.

The interior of Daisy's car in the police garage. *Courtesy of the Michigan State Police.*

Two were on the inside rearview mirror, left probably from someone adjusting it. Another was on the interior chrome strip on the right front seat.

As the troopers crawled through the car, they checked the driver's side door. There was another fingerprint at the back end of the armrest pull. This one stood out. If someone had been driving the car, this was where he would have pulled the door shut.

The detailed check of the car went on until 3:00 a.m. with the troopers checking for any other fibers, hairs or fingerprints. Even with the space heater running, it was cold work in the garage as they tried to find anything that would help them identify the killer.

Detective Conn noted what was *not* there: Daisy's keys. Floyd had test started the car on Michigan Avenue using his set of keys. Daisy's were missing, meaning that her killer had taken them either inadvertently or as some sort of souvenir of the crime. A check was made with Floyd. Daisy had a simple split key ring. She had two sets of keys for the Pontiac, one house key and one that was for her locker at Kellogg's.

Police felt certain that someone must have seen the car or the driver on Michigan Avenue. It was one of the busiest pieces of roadway in Calhoun County. Despite the cold, it had been broad daylight. Whoever had killed Daisy had driven the car and deliberately abandoned it. The person would have been covered in blood splatters. Ralph Kartheu pointed out that if the killer had been wearing yellow cotton gloves, as suspected, they would have been soaked in blood. The investigators began to comb the area around Evanston Road and East Michigan Avenue in the hope of finding someone who had seen the driver or the vehicle.

On the morning of January 14, 1963, Sergeant Fred Ritchie of the Calhoun County Sheriff's Department had been late on his way to court to transport a prisoner. He reached the courthouse by driving on Michigan Avenue. As he came up the hill near Evanston Road, he had spotted the white Pontiac Bonneville. The extreme cold weather had killed a number of cars that morning, so the sight of a car on the side of the road was not unusual. Fred saw a single man in a blue coat, what looked like a navy peacoat, walking toward Battle Creek not far from the car. Fred didn't check the time or get a good look at the man; he was more focused on being late for court. Little did he realize at the time that he had passed Daisy Zick's murderer.

Sharon Brown's home at 1189 East Michigan Avenue was where the car had been abandoned. When the troopers first visited her, she claimed that she had seen the vehicle at approximately 10:30 a.m. The car had been parked in such a way to force her to walk around it to get her mail that morning. Mrs. Brown recalled the time so well because she had been talking to a neighbor on the telephone, and after hanging up, she had looked at the clock. Shortly thereafter she had seen the car in front of her home. A few days after her initial report of the time, she contacted the investing officers to revise her stated time. Some minutes had passed between when she had noted the time and when she had first seen the Pontiac. She estimated that she had seen the car closer to 11:00 a.m.

The police made a check of the Dog 'n Suds on the other side of the street less than a quarter of a mile from where the car had been abandoned. The

Dog n' Suds was primarily a drive-in restaurant during the summer months and had a small interior eating area. Winters were the bane of drive-in restaurants, as their business dropped off dramatically. Dressie Lampkin had been working that day, filling in for her sister, who usually worked at that time. She remembered only one customer during that time: a man who came in, left and, later, returned. He came back at 11:30 a.m., just as she was leaving for the day. He was a white male, in light tan-colored clothing. He wore a topcoat. She remembered him because he flirted with her. Dressie did not notice anything out of the ordinary about him. There was no sign of blood on him.

The Brown house, where Daisy's car was abandoned. *Courtesy of the Michigan State Police.*

The view of where Daisy's car was located, from Sharon Brown's house. *Courtesy of the Michigan State Police.*

Other neighbors provided little more in the way of details. Donna Brooker of Evanston Street did not see the car at 9:55 a.m. but did see it at 12:10 p.m. She hadn't seen anyone walking about that morning. The Steen family—Ed, Beth and their two boys—saw the Zick Bonneville at 11:00 a.m., they were fairly sure. Pinning down the exact time the car arrived was proving to be difficult. Earl and Doris McIntire on Palmer Street left home at 11:00 a.m. and didn't see the

The view from where Daisy's car was parked on East Michigan Avenue, facing east. *Courtesy of the Michigan State Police.*

The view from where Daisy's car was discovered looking west on Michigan Avenue toward Battle Creek. *Courtesy of the Michigan State Police.*

car, for example, but Carl Hoff of Hoff's Gulf Station said he saw the car around 10:30 a.m. near Evanston road, though he didn't see anyone there.

Mrs. Maude Brooker on Evanston Street saw a light grey or tan car parked between her house and East Michigan Avenue near the mailboxes. It was there until around noon, when she noticed it was gone. Was this the killer's vehicle, positioned so that he could make his getaway?

As the police combed the area around Juno Street and Wattles Road, more information emerged. Mrs. Beulah Hankey of Wattles Road claimed that she passed the Zick car being driven north on Wattles Road between 11:20 a.m. to 11:30 a.m. She was with Mrs. Habenicht, another neighbor who was able to substantiate this story. Mrs. Hankey felt her estimate of the time was accurate because Mrs. Habenicht left her home at 11:20 a.m. after giving her young son medication for a heart condition. Little did Mrs. Hankey realize that Daisy's killer was behind the wheel.

The day after the murder, the *Enquirer and News* picked up one tip. An unidentified source said that on the morning of the murder, his car had stalled on Michigan Avenue, almost across from where Daisy's car came to rest. He claimed that another car, "bluish in color," had been parked behind Daisy's Pontiac. A man got out of Daisy's car and got into the passenger seat of the blue car and the driver took off.

This sighting, if accurate, would have helped immensely. It meant that two persons were involved with the murder, the killer and the driver of the final getaway car. But this witness's story didn't hold water. First, there were a number of witnesses who saw Daisy's car that morning, but none saw the other mysterious blue car or the anonymous witness's vehicle. Also, several people saw the supposed driver of the car walking along Michigan Avenue, heading west. If this had been the killer, he couldn't have been seen walking if he had already hopped into a car and fled with an accomplice.

Detective Conn couldn't simply disregard the account, however, especially since the story had already run in the newspaper. He tracked down the informant, and after a few minutes of questioning, the man admitted that he had made up the entire account of a second man in the car. He couldn't say why he had lied about the story. He then said that he had seen another young man in the area hitchhiking that day, not far from where Daisy's car had been abandoned.

Conn tracked down the twenty-nine-year-old man who had been seen hitchhiking in the vicinity. The man in question raised a number of eyebrows. He had previously been caught breaking into a woman's home and rummaging through her lingerie. He had also been arrested before for making an indecent proposal to an unsuspecting housewife who had answered his knock at the door. In Conn's mind, this could potentially be the same scenario that Daisy had faced. Maybe she had simply made the mistake of opening the door for him.

The hopes of the investigators were shattered when the man permitted being questioned under a polygraph exam and passed. He appeared to be a dead-end, but Conn remained convinced that the young man might be involved despite the results of the test.

Harper Creek High School had been contacted to see if there had been any absent students that day from the Wattles Park area. It was not a good day for boys to be playing hooky. Jim Fitzjohn, Art English and Bill Adams were out of school that day with unexcused absences, and the police visited all of them to see where they had been and if they had seen anything.

Another team of state troopers turned their focus on the neighborhood where the Zicks lived. What police learned was that tiny little Juno Street had been abuzz with activity the day of the crime, yet few people saw anything of use to the investigators. Margaret Simpson at 124 Juno had called Glenn White Heating to repair her furnace. It had conked out on the coldest day of the year. The deep-penetrating cold had caused a spike of calls for furnace repairs in the area. Two heating repairmen, Robert Lee and Richard Burning, were assigned the task of going to the Simpson house the morning of the murder, putting them on the street near the time of the killing.

Prosecutor Noble Moore had both men come in for questioning. Richard Burning lived on Wattles Road and knew the neighborhood, so it was hoped he might have picked up on some minute details of anything out of the ordinary. Burning carefully reconstructed his day for the officers. He and Robert Lee had another call that morning at the Friends Church parsonage on Katherine Street, only a few blocks away from where Daisy's car had been abandoned.

Having finished at the church, the two repairmen had arrived on Juno Street around 9:30 a.m. It had taken them roughly a half hour to get the Simpson furnace working. Neither had seen anything peculiar or out of place.

The furnace repairmen were not alone in the sweep of people visiting near Juno Street that morning. An oil deliveryman was tracked down as well. He had been making a delivery at a home on Wattles Road, just off Juno Street, at around 10:00 a.m. Like so many people that day, he didn't see anyone walking in the cold.

The police contacted two local dairies that did milk delivery in the area. Though milkmen were a dying breed in the age of the supermarket—Steve's Wattles Park Grocery was only a block and a half away from the Zick home, and a half dozen other markets were within five miles—there were still some holdouts that had their milk delivered. However, neither company had deliveries in that area the day of the murder.

Betty Habenicht had arranged for heating oil to be delivered that morning. With the icy weather, no one wanted to run out of oil. The deliveryman, Mr. Lloyd Eakins of Battle Creek, arrived at her home between 11:00 and 11:30 a.m. He told investigators that he didn't see a car or person on Juno Street. He did remember seeing Mrs. DeFrance walking toward her mailbox. It stood out in his mind because her dog barked and chased his truck when he left. Mr. Eakins was a little confused why the police asked what kind of gloves he had been wearing that day. When he pumped oil, he usually wore red cloth gloves for heat and pulled on a pair of black rubber gloves over them.

Eakins's story matched up with that of Mrs. DeFrance, who provided the police with a description of the man she had seen across the street at the Zick home that morning. When pressed for details of the man she saw, she could only offer a generic description. The alleged killer stood about five feet seven inches and weighed about 135 pounds. From what she could tell from across the street and from behind, he was probably in his late twenties or early thirties. The man had been wearing a blue denim–type jacket with lighter blue pants and had black or dark hair but no hat. From what Mrs. DeFrance could see, he was a white man.

Another person who was in the area at the time was Mae Tolls, the cleaning woman who was working at the Radford home across the street from the Zick home that morning. When she went out to shake the rugs at around 9:30 a.m., she noticed that Mrs. Zick had pulled the drapes open around that time, which was unusual for her. Daisy usually didn't do that until around 11:00 a.m.

Lieutenant Paul Scoder of the Battle Creek Police Department tracked down the cab companies in town to see if they had picked up anyone in the vicinity. The killer had to have had a way out of the Wattles Park area after abandoning the Zick Pontiac; perhaps he had taken a cab. Only one fare came from the Wattles Park area that day, a woman who was taken to the Post Tavern—a bar in downtown Battle Creek.

Running down the list of people who might have been in the neighborhood at the time of the killing, the police contacted the postal deliveryman, William Newman Daily. Daily said that at 10:05 a.m., he had been driving past the Chuck Wagon Restaurant, going east on Michigan Avenue. The Chuck Wagon was approximately a mile west from where the Zicks' Pontiac had been abandoned.

According to Daily, he saw a white male walking west on Michigan Avenue. The man looked around forty years old, standing five foot five or five foot eight inches tall, with black hair. From what Daily claimed, the man was bare-headed and weighed from 150 to 170 pounds. He had been wearing a black waist-length jacket like a gabardine. Daily claimed that the man had a dark complexion. He also stated that the man he had seen had a peculiar grin on his face, like he was smiling to himself.

Daily said that the Zicks were on his mail route and he had gone past their house at approximately 11:10 a.m. When he went past the home, he was sure that the garage door was closed. He volunteered to the officers that the car was usually pulled in straight in the garage and backed out when someone left. According to him, Daisy usually backed it out and left the engine running while she closed the garage door.

The only other witness that came forward in the early part of the investigation in regard to the car was Trooper Ralph Kartheu, who had been one of the first officers dispatched to the Zick home. He had been on patrol before 11:00 a.m., passed Daisy's car and noticed someone behind the wheel. He had gotten a good look at the person there, Floyd Zick. Trooper Kartheu substantiated this much of Floyd's story—that he had stopped to try starting Daisy's car. Little did Trooper Kartheu realize that in a few short minutes he would see the man again at Zick's home on Juno Street.

Detective Conn's team was faced with the usual problems with witnesses and times. There was always a lot of variance in times as people remembered them. Slowly though, a pattern was emerging. At some time after 10:20 a.m. and just before 11:00 a.m., Daisy's killer was driving her car from the scene of the crime to where it was abandoned near the Dog 'n Suds at Michigan Avenue and Evanston Road. The individual left the car and, after a few short minutes, disappeared.

William Daily's vivid account of a man walking on Michigan Avenue was one of the wildcards. He claimed that when he had delivered on his route, the Zicks' garage door was closed, which certainly wasn't the case at 11:00 a.m. He seemed fairly aware of Daisy's routine and seemed sure of the time of day when he had been in the area. He was the only one who saw the mysterious man walking near the Chuck Wagon.

The confidential informant's account of seeing a car pull up to take the driver of Daisy's car away certainly made sense, but no one else had reported seeing that informant's car or the other car along the road that morning. Photos of Daisy's vehicle were released to the *Enquirer and News* to see if anyone had seen anyone or anything of interest, but none could confirm the account provided. Credible witnesses, such as Sergeant Fred Ritchie, only described a single man walking along Michigan Avenue in the stinging cold that morning.

Where did the blood-covered killer walk to that morning? If he had been wearing a dark blue navy peacoat, it would have been harder to see the stains until you were up close. Regardless of its visibility on his coat, blood would have been on his lighter pants as well.

Police were going to have to wait to see if any additional witnesses came forward. Daisy's Bonneville had yielded all the clues it had to offer at that point in time.

Prosecutor Noble Moore called a conference the second day of the investigation to attempt to go over the evidence and clues that had been gathered up to that point. Leads were starting to trickle in, but nothing with results had yet been found. "Now we have to sit down and see if any of the leads add up to certain persons on whom we can concentrate."

A description of the man that Mrs. DeFrance had seen was released to the public, if not to provoke identification, at least to calm its fears. To

The view down Juno Street toward Wattles Road. The Zick home is on the left with the state police car in the driveway. *Courtesy of the Michigan State Police.*

Mrs. DeFrance's horror, her name was also released to the newspapers. She became very concerned that the murderer knew that he had been seen, and now her name and address had been printed in the *Battle Creek Enquirer and News* for the whole world to read. According to one neighbor, "Mrs. DeFrance was petrified that the killer would come after her to keep her quiet."

Many of the neighbors on Juno Street and nearby neighborhoods were nervous that the killer might strike again. Myrtle Evans was a young housewife on Wattles Road whose driveway opened up to Juno Street. Myrtle recalled the day of the murder: "I was a young mother with four children. One was ill with tonsillitis; the youngest had to go with us to the doctor in Jackson County. When I returned home, the neighborhood was swarming with police cars, that's when I learned about Daisy…my husband worked nights, and I was a nervous wreck. I went to my cousin's in Jackson County for a couple of nights, then my father-in-law came and stayed for about two weeks."

Having a murder strike such a pastoral community shook many families' calm and sent ripples of fear into their homes.

In the meantime, Detective Conn contacted Daisy's work, the Kellogg's Factory in Battle Creek. He went to recover the affects from Daisy's locker, optimistic that there would be some clue or clues as to who might want her dead.

Her locker proved a boon for the investigators. Most of its contents were the mundane articles that any female factory worker might have: a hand mirror, a can of Cashmere Bouquet talcum powder, a can of Breck hair set mist, a multicolored umbrella, a shoe horn, white tape, a gray and aqua sweater, three calendars, shoe polish, roll-on deodorant, a spool of white thread, scissors, a marking pencil, a scarf and five slips. However, there were other items that caught the detective's attention. Two gift-wrapped packages addressed to "Raymond Honey" were in the locker, and there were numerous notes and cards—all of a romantic nature.

The items uncovered in Daisy's locker and the statements of her friend Audrey gave investigators a set of clues that would take the them into the corporate culture of the Kellogg Company and the sex life of Daisy Zick.

Chapter 4
THE AFFAIRS OF DAISY ZICK

I had a good life and loved my mom.

Jim King
Daisy's son

I f you want to know about the personality of a person, you have to understand the culture in which they were raised and where they lived. We are all the products of our surroundings, and that was especially true of Daisy Zick. The city she worked in governed her life. It determined whom she met, worked with and associated with. To know Daisy as a person, you have to look at where she lived, her life history and the place where she spent so much of her time—the Kellogg Company.

At one point or another in our nation's history, everywhere was considered the frontier of the United States. In 1823–24, that frontier was western Michigan. To mark the wilderness for settling, teams of surveyors were sent out from Fort Detroit. One such team set up its camp along the river known by the local Indians as Waupokisco, meaning River of Battle or River of Blood, which commemorated a great battle fought on its banks years before the white settlers came. This river met with a larger river, named the Kalamazoo, and it was at this juncture that the surveying team led by Colonel John Mullet had set up its camp.

The local Indians, at first, were simply onlookers to the group's work, but over time, they began to interfere with the work being done by standing to block the surveyors' lines of sight. Colonel Mullet became so enraged that, on one occasion, he took his Jacob's staff (an iron rod on which the surveyor placed his compass) and attempted to run through one of the natives who was interfering with his work. Only the swift action of a Frenchman attached to the party prevented the incident from being one of bloodshed. It was becoming clear to both parties that conflict was inevitable.

One day, while the surveying party was working, two men from the camp—a cook named Taylor and another man named Edwin Baldwin—were attacked by two large Indians. The assumed motive was robbery, but the white settlers fought back. The Indian fighting Baldwin managed to grab Colonel Mullet's musket and fired the weapon. Baldwin was narrowly missed, the musket ball tearing a hole in his coat. Baldwin seized the rifle from his assailant and clubbed him about the head with it. Meanwhile, Taylor was on the verge of being overpowered, when Baldwin came in and killed Taylor's attacker with another blow from the musket. Realizing it was far from security, the survey party retreated to Detroit. What it left behind was the name that the Waupokisco River and the community that would settle there would adopt as its own: Battle Creek.

Battle Creek was formally founded six years after the surveyor-Indian scuffle, when Sands McCamly purchased the first plots of land for a dollar and a quarter an acre. The early settlers' names still resound in the streets, parks and neighborhoods of Battle Creek—McCamly, Convis, Wattles, Ethridge, Harper, Willard, Kingman, Browning, Crosby and others. The position of the settlement near the middle of the state's east–west Territorial Road made it a perfect resting place for travelers. During the Civil War, Battle Creek sent its sons off to fight for both sides of the conflict. It became a station on the Underground Railroad, helping slaves escape to freedom. Sojourner Truth, the famous escaped slave and advocate for women's rights, made Battle Creek her home in later life.

The city grew as the state of Michigan grew. The Michigan Central Railroad pushed through the heart of the city in 1845, bringing with it more settlers and more business. While the city emerged as the largest community in Calhoun County, it was not the seat of county government, which resided eight miles down Michigan Avenue in quaint, bustling little Marshall. The surrounding lush farmlands were celebrated for raising wheat and corn. But like many small cities, Battle Creek would need a catalyst to make it thrive and become recognized. Usually this catalyst comes in the form of a business that brings people and jobs into a community. For Battle Creek, that catalyst came initially in the form of a church, but it would eventually lead to changing how the world ate their morning breakfast.

Today, Battle Creek is known as "Cereal City," but that title emerged from the Church of Seventh Day Adventists rather than an oven. Battle Creek became the founding city for the religion. One of the distinctions of the Seventh Day Adventists was their belief in nutrition as a way to purify the body and spirit of a person. Good health was an important principle to the members of the church and leading this nutritional reform was one of the church's founders, Mrs. Ellen White. She encouraged and helped fund sending a young Adventist, John Harvey Kellogg, to college to become a doctor.

Dr. Kellogg took over the Adventists' health institute, reorganizing it into the Battle Creek Sanitarium. There, he experimented with and tested a wide range of foods to determine their benefits on patients. Dr. Kellogg advocated the use of grains and cereals at the sanitarium, or the "San" as it became known. He made granola for patients for a breakfast food and experimented with yogurts and other cereals. Patients from around the world came to Battle Creek not just for the headquarters of the Seventh Day Adventists but also to spend time at the San. It became a resort for the rich and famous coming to Battle Creek.

With Dr. John Kellogg focused on experimenting with nutrition, he needed his brother, Will, to help manage the business side of his operation. The brothers were far from close. As their sister Emma put it, "The Kellogg women are amenable, but the Kellogg men can be *mean.*" John ran his brother ragged in keeping the San a viable operation.

In 1894, Dr. Kellogg changed the world in a subtle way. While attempting to come up with a viable food for a patient who had false teeth and could not chew well, he boiled some wheat and ran it through a press before baking the flattened material in his oven. The first true breakfast cereal was born. Kellogg had not only devised the means of providing a nutritious breakfast food but also found a way of taking the corn and wheat that farmers had been growing in mid-Michigan and dramatically increasing their commercial value. Battle Creek spawned a new industry, and Kellogg created a magnificent redbrick plant along the Michigan Central Railroad line so that its products could easily be distributed to Chicago to the west and Detroit to the east.

One of the San's former patients, Charlie Post, saw the benefits of the foods that Dr. Kellogg made. He created his own natural coffee substitute, Postum, which he had allegedly proposed to Dr. Kellogg only to have the good doctor turn him down. Postum, thanks to a brilliant marketing campaign, became a nationwide hit. The byproducts of this grain-made coffee became a new breakfast cereal, Grape-Nuts. Post, too, set up his production facility in Battle Creek. While Kellogg claimed that Post had stolen his concepts from the San, Post seemed to be ever defiant that his creations were his own. The two plants were set up within a block of each other, locked in marketing combat for decades to come.

Seemingly overnight, Battle Creek had become a boomtown for the cereal business. Anyone attempting to get into this new market seemed compelled to set up his operations in the growing city. Healthy breakfasts became synonymous with Battle Creek. Countless products sprang up from the two large manufacturers and the dozens of smaller companies that sprouted in "Cereal City." As the comedy magazine *Jabs* put it, "Battle Creek, Michigan, has a population of 21,647 persons, all of whom are engaged in the manufacturer of breakfast cereals."

Inevitably, the Kellogg brothers were to come to blows over the business. With the introduction of Toasted Corn Flakes, the brothers finally began a legal battle for control of the company. For a while, the two ran opposing businesses, but eventually, the younger W.K. Kellogg managed to purchase and consolidate the holdings into the one Kellogg Company that is known today. Dr. John Kellogg still spent much of his time at the San, but by the Great Depression, the stream of celebrity visitors to Battle Creek had dwindled to a mere trickle. The bitter sibling quarrels of the Kellogg brothers were often overshadowed by the fierce competition between Kellogg's and Post. The companies played a constant game of chess to out-maneuver and out-market each other.

Battle Creek was transformed by the cereal business, as it brought in jobs, fostered a boom in agriculture in the Midwest and put Battle Creek on the world map as the birthplace of healthy breakfasts. Even in the 1950s, when the trend was to turn breakfast cereals into sugar-laden treats rather than nutritious food, the town still wore its mantle of "Cereal City" with pride. By the 1950s, Kellogg's had become a corporate giant. General Mills and Ralston Purina had factories in the city as well. W.K. Kellogg's legacy, the Kellogg Foundation, was also based in Battle Creek. While there were other industrial plants in the city such as Union Pump, it was the breakfast industry that defined the place.

The Battle Creek of 1963 was not all that different than the city is today. The railroads that bring in supplies and transport breakfast out to the world cut around and through the city. Most locals will tell you that if you wanted to get from one side of Battle Creek to the other you had better add fifteen minutes to account for being stopped by a slow-moving train. Even as far out as Wattles Park, the mournful diesel horns echo in the evenings. Many residents can tell which cereal lines were running at Kellogg's by the aroma in the air. Cornflakes had a soothing smell whereas burned Rice Krispies made you cringe. Fruit Loops left a sugary taste on your palate.

In 1963, Battle Creek was a city overshadowed by the businesses that made it. Its identity was not its own but driven, instead, by Post and Kellogg's. And the cereal companies defined not only the town but also the people that lived there.

———•·•———

Police officers look at murder victims differently than authors or historians. They dig into their past looking for possible suspects—relationships with possible murderers. They seek individuals with motives to kill someone in the present, not looking into the whole life story of the victim. To really understand Daisy Zick, you need to understand her as a person rather than a label of "a party girl" or a "loose woman."

Daisy Holmes (later Zick) was born February 5, 1919, on a farm in Assyria township near Hastings, Michigan. She was born to Gaylord Charles Holmes and his wife, Pearl A. (Woods) Holmes. Her father's family had been from Ohio in the 1850s but had moved to the Hastings area in the 1880s. They had been there ever since. Daisy's parents, Gaylord and Pearl, had been married in Battle Creek in 1918 in a tiny service attended by the bride's parents. They took their honeymoon on his Assyria Township farm.

Daisy's father had farming in his blood. He had worked for a short period of time as a road commissioner in Assyria Township in the early 1900s and then as a blacksmith, but in the end, farming was what spoke to him. He had registered for the draft for the Great War but had never been called up. While he dabbled in carpentry, he set up his family on a farm on Mud Lake Road, and the place became the center of their world.

Assyria Township is a rural community surrounded by the towns of Battle Creek, Charlotte and Hastings. The citizens tend to see themselves as part of the Hastings community since the township is in a different county (Barry) than Battle Creek. Hastings is poised on the wandering Thornapple River, situated north of Battle Creek and west of Lansing. Hastings is the county seat of Barry County and had become a city more because of its positioning as a potential stagecoach stop than any other reason. Lumber had been a big business in the area in its early years, but that shifted to agriculture as time passed. Hastings has an incredibly quaint Victorian feel in its architecture and appearance.

The city's position near Grand Rapids, Lansing, Battle Creek and Kalamazoo offered its residents numerous employment opportunities. It had two tiny movie theaters, the Strand and the Barry. The cinema is one of the few forms of entertainment that linked the locals to the outside world. As the municipal center of Barry County, Hastings was a hub of activity. The end of summer was always marked with the Barry County Fair. Downtown Hastings had redbrick roads, which gave cars and trucks passing over them a distinct rumble.

The Holmes family were farmers, and Daisy was born on the family-owned farm. Her sister, Dorothy, was also born there, in 1921. The farm was ten to twelve miles outside Battle Creek. The Holmes family was hardworking. Daisy's father had lived on a farm his whole life in a rental arrangement, and when the farm came up for sale, he purchased it as his own. The Holmes family was not rich but was by no means poor.

For schooling, Daisy attended a one-room schoolhouse called Eagle. She completed the eighth grade, which for the late 1920s was considered a good education. The fact that she didn't attend high school was not surprising, as many of the rural citizens of Barry County, Michigan, only went as far as their one-room schoolhouses allowed.

Daisy and her sister, Dorothy, 1925. *Courtesy of James King.*

Daisy's world was small. There simply weren't a lot of opportunities to meet people that didn't live beyond where you could walk or ride to. She met an older man named Neville "Bill" King, who lived only three-quarters of a mile down the road from the Holmes farm. He was twenty-two years old, and when she met him in 1933, she was only fourteen. Despite the differences in their ages, Daisy was swept off her feet. Today, the concept of a fourteen-year-old marrying an older man would be the fodder talk, but it was not entirely out of the ordinary in the 1930s. They went down to Angola, Indiana, and were married by a Reverend Davies on September 29, 1933. Neville's family was from the region, and the marriage laws were more flexible there.

Daisy, a young farm girl, in 1930. *Courtesy of James King.*

Neville worked at the United Steel and Wire Company in Battle Creek, making slightly less than thirty dollars a week, a good wage for the period. Shortly after they married, he moved from Hastings to Battle Creek, taking his young bride with him. They moved into a house on North Division Street in the city limits. Together, Daisy and Neville had a son, James (Jim), born on April 1, 1936. Daisy was seventeen when James was born. James's birth was fine, but the boy was born with a birthmark on his face, a dark pink, almost purple, coloration.

Daisy's life with Neville was not the idyllic one that she had hoped for or deserved. Neville was cruel to his young wife. While she had been pregnant with Jim, she had left Neville for her parents' home. She didn't stay away long though, eventually returning to Battle Creek and her husband.

To characterize Neville as abusive was to be kind. His abuse of Daisy was not just physical. He "call[ed] her vile, indecent and sacrilegious names," erupting with the slightest provocation. He often struck her in anger. He twisted Daisy's wrists and, on more than one occasion, kicked her. Records from the divorce filings reveal that Neville "ha[d] otherwise

Daisy and her first husband, Neville King. *Courtesy of James King.*

beaten plaintiff (Daisy) to an extent that is difficult to believe a husband would beat his wife, that on one occasion he struck plaintiff a violent blow upon her nose and broke the plaintiff's nose," causing her pain and suffering for days afterward. His explosions of rage were so loud that neighbors and passersby could hear and, in the case of the neighbors, complain.

Neville's rage against Daisy was so strong that on one occasion he threatened to kill her. For her, that had been the breaking point. She had taken James and had returned to Hastings and her family.

Divorce in the 1930s was not as commonplace as today, and exacting details of offenses had to be documented by the courts. Furthermore, since she was under the age of twenty-one, Daisy was declared an "infant" in the eyes of the court. They went through formal proceedings to have her father named as her "Next Friend," entitling him to sue for the divorce for his daughter. At the age of eighteen, young Daisy had been through a tough life already, experiencing what many people do not experience in an entire lifetime.

The divorce ended with Neville being required to pay three dollars a week for support of James and to pay the costs of James's treatments at the University of Michigan hospital to attempt to correct his birthmark. Like many divorces, Daisy's did not end cleanly. Neville was entitled to visitations on Sundays and on key holidays. When he showed up on Sundays, however, the Holmes family simply wasn't at home. When he confronted Daisy's father, his former father-in-law threatened to "lick" him. Neville had to go back to court to enforce his rights to see his son.

Daisy did not simply stay at her parents' farm to raise her son; she went to work to provide for him. In 1936, Daisy took a job at the Nabisco Biscuit Company in Battle Creek. At that time, Battle Creek had over a dozen cereal companies attempting to seize a piece of the business that Post and Kellogg's were carving out of the breakfast market. When she started at Nabisco, Daisy began commuting from the farm to work. While it was only a twelve-mile commute each way, in 1936, some of the roads were still dirt and those that were paved were often rough. Such a commute put a lot of wear and tear on a vehicle.

Daisy's sister, Dorothy, worked at the competing Western Biscuit Company in Battle Creek. The two girls decided that it would save them money to simply get an apartment in the city. For Daisy, this forced a decision in regard to her son, James. Having him live in the apartment was impractical given that he was still young and needed supervision. The agreement arranged with her parents was that they would take care of James during the week, and on the weekends, Daisy would return to the farm to spend time with him. When the weekend was over, Daisy would drive back to Battle Creek for another week of work. It was a pattern that lasted through the 1940s.

One can only imagine the strain that Daisy felt being away from her son five days at a time, though she sometimes made trips home during the week as well. Daisy eventually changed jobs to work at Kellogg's on the night shift. At the time, the cereal maker ran four shifts, six hours each. Payday at Kellogg's was every Thursday. Without fail, she would cash her paycheck and purchase a little toy for Jim before driving out to the family farm. When he woke up on Friday mornings, there was always a present from his mother waiting for him. Daisy, like many of the workers at Kellogg's, also managed to secure the free prizes and toys that were packaged in the cereal boxes. In Battle Creek, employees often brought home the toys packaged with the cereal for their children. Daisy would always leave these small prizes for Jim, who would take them to school and hand them out, making him a popular kid.

When World War II erupted, Battle Creek became a hub of wartime activity. The cereal industry became packagers of prepared foods for soldiers. Numerous other businesses focused on wartime production emerged. Fort Custer became an active training base, bringing thousands of service personnel through Battle Creek as well as the businesses (bars) that pried the pay from these new soldiers. Overnight the seemingly quiet city of Battle Creek was transformed to a bustling city.

Daisy and her son Jim during World War II.
Courtesy of James King.

It was during this period that a different Daisy emerged. Daisy became a "party gal," according to her son, Jim. She had been dating a man steadily from Hastings, but he had been called up for military service and left. Her time alone was short-lived. The war brought thousands of men into Battle Creek and broadened her opportunities to meet other men. Dances became popular in the city, and Daisy became a regular at such events. Daisy dated a number of men at the start of the war. In an environment in which the number of men dramatically outnumbered the women, there were a number of wartime romances.

It was in this environment that she met Floyd Zick.

Floyd Zick was born in Denzer, Wisconsin. He was enlisted in the army in late 1941, and his training brought him to Fort Custer in Battle Creek. Floyd and Daisy began to date after being regulars at dances. They fell in love and prepared to get married, and both of them wanted to do what was right for her son, Jim. When they announced that they were getting married, they sat down with him and discussed his options. He could remain on the farm that had been his boyhood home with his grandparents and with his mother visiting him; or he could move in with Floyd and Daisy. He made the choice to stay on the farm.

After the war, Floyd was employed as a "meat manager," more commonly known as a butcher, at Fales' Market. He had started out working for Al Fales when Fales opened the East End Market in Post Edition and had stayed with him when the market moved to the Main Street location. He was a playful and friendly man, though it was well known that Floyd was a heavy drinker. Marie Fales, the young daughter of the owner, would go into the market Saturdays to listen to the *Big John and Sparky* radio program that he played on the radio in the meat department. Her strongest memory of Floyd was that he loved to make people laugh. By most accounts, he was engaging and outgoing.

Jim remained close to his mother even after her marriage. On Saturdays, his grandmother would give him $1.50, and he would hitchhike into Battle Creek to go to the shows. There were seven theaters in town, and he would hit all of them before going to spend the rest of the day with his mom, staying at her apartment on Kingman Avenue. Daisy would then drive him home on Sunday and spend the day with the family.

Daisy and Floyd were very social and liked to go out dancing. They went to St. Mary's Lake, White Rabbit and Fine Lake, where dance clubs and halls hosted local bands. Sometimes they took Jim with them, and he would hang with the other kids there while his mother and stepfather danced.

Right, top and bottom: Floyd and Daisy Zick during happier times, around 1945. *Courtesy of James King.*

Floyd, Jim and Daisy together. *Courtesy of James King.*

Daisy with her son, Jim, and her granddaughter, Lori. *Courtesy of James King.*

Her years with Floyd were among some of the happiest of her life. She had a stable home life and had seemed to put some of her past behind her. Floyd went fishing with Jim on several occasions, though they never became close. Jim became the first member of his family to graduate high school in Hastings and got a job as a surveyor's helper. Jim met his future wife, Ruth Ann ("Ruthie"), who lived in his neighborhood. Daisy was really excited to help plan their wedding in 1957, holding the rehearsal dinner at the Wagon Wheel Restaurant near her home in Battle Creek.

Ruthie became pregnant in 1959, and Daisy was not excited at the prospect at first. At the age of forty, Daisy felt that she was too young to become a grandmother. She eventually warmed up to the idea, and when her granddaughter Lori was born, Daisy quickly embraced her new role in life.

Things were not all sunshine and roses at the Zick home however. Floyd's drinking increased. He was not a dysfunctional alcoholic, but he was known to drink often. As the 1950s wore on, Daisy began to have affairs with other men. As one investigator on her case put it, "Daisy's always portrayed as being a loose woman, but our digging into the case indicated that she dated one man steady before moving on to the next." From what the police found in their research, her relationships seemed to be longer term—at least a month or two at time—and monogamous. Jim's own recollection was that Daisy had a lot of boyfriends. He caught her several times with them, passing them in his car or seeing her with a man who was not her husband at a bar.

Of course, with the passage of time, more of Daisy's affairs have become known, driven and fed by the publicity of her death. One person told me the story of how her mother went to a bar a month before Daisy's murder to confront her about the affair her husband was allegedly having with the vivacious redhead. While not pertinent to the case, it does cast doubt on the police theory that Daisy was only dating one man at a time. It is conceivable that she had a number of suitors. As one neighbor put it, "There's always cars over at the Zick home." Battle Creek, while a small city, was not small enough to keep such affairs secret. Per Jim's recollection, "I don't know if Floyd knew or not. I have to believe he did."

Daisy fishing and enjoying life, 1949. *Courtesy of James King.*

The investigators who are still alive tend to agree that Floyd had to have known about his wife's affairs. She was not secretive. Her car was parked at bars when she was on the town, not hidden a few blocks away. Her flirtations were common knowledge to her co-workers and with others in town. People talked behind her back about her affairs, but if this bothered her, she didn't let on. Daisy was a free spirit and didn't let other people govern her actions. By 1963 standards, this was shocking, but given the free love culture of the late 1960s, Daisy was simply a trailblazer.

At the same time, officers knew that Daisy was not the only person in the house having an affair: Floyd was suspected of at least one as well. One former Battle Creek police officer stated it this way: "Floyd was seeing a girl over on Calhoun Street. I saw him going to visit her several times, and it was well known in town."

Daisy's lifestyle became the focus of the investigation into her death. A scorned lover or jealous wife might just hold enough resentment to commit murder. The discovery of the knife with a hint of blood on it that most likely came from Kellogg's steered investigators to Kellogg's, specifically Daisy's lover at the time of her death, Raymond Mercer. As the investigators put it: "It has been ascertained that victim has been a woman of questioned reputation for a long period of time and possibly has jilted suitors or jealous suitors in her background. Considerable time will be spent on developing information from the Kellogg factory."

While teams of investigators combed Kellogg's for more information, others were still attempting to search for the murder weapon. Though the examiner had ruled out the Spoilage knife during the autopsy, most investigators felt it was the murder weapon. Nevertheless, when Jim King, Daisy's son, arrived from New York, he was pressed into helping Trooper Ralph Kartheu search the rafters in the garage for a potential weapon.

Back at the factory, the thirty-nine-year-old Mercer had been dating Daisy for almost two years. He himself was married. As her current love interest, Mercer went under an immense amount of immediate scrutiny from investigators. Mercer claimed that he had been working at the time of the murder and had no reason whatsoever to kill Daisy. His timecard could validate where he was, but as anyone in Battle Creek knew, timecard fraud was rampant at the cereal factory. Friends and co-workers often punched in people who were late, and employees sometimes didn't punch out for lunch.

Investigators met with Earl Latimer, David Armstrong and Joe Noga, all of whom worked on the conveyor line with Mercer on the day of the murder. David Armstrong said that the group broke for lunch at 10:40 a.m.

but that he hadn't seen Mercer in the cafeteria. He had assumed that Mercer had gone to the Soda Bar for lunch. By 11:20 a.m., Mercer was back on the job, though Joe noticed that he seemed nervous. Investigators asked how his clothing appeared, and Armstrong said that Mercer was wearing the same attire that he had in the morning.

Earl Latimer and his brother were at the Soda Bar for lunch and didn't see Mercer there. At 10:40 a.m., Joe Noga had seen Mercer taking an elevator headed up in the plant. Dale Mapes, Mercer's supervisor, stated that he was not always present where his crew was working but that he had seen Mercer during the lunch break.

To the investigators this seemed disappointing. Mercer would not have had enough time to leave the plant, park some distance from the Zick home, walk to it, kill Daisy, walk back to his car and get back to work without being noticed. While it was possible to leave the plant and commit the crime, the 10:40 a.m. timing did not match up with the timing that Mrs. DeFrance gave of seeing the murderer at the breezeway of the Zick home.

Mercer was cooperative with the investigators. He had called Daisy at 9:00 a.m. the morning she had been killed. His break had been short, and he estimated that they had spoken for around twelve minutes. There was nothing out of the ordinary in her behavior or tone. She had told him that she was going to meet with Audrey Heminger at 10:30 a.m. and that she was just getting ready to take her bath. In order to help the investigators, Mercer agreed to take a polygraph test and provide his fingerprints. One of his prints was found on the mirror in Daisy's car, but given that he had been dating Daisy, this alone was not enough to consider him a suspect. The results of his polygraph indicated that he did not have any involvement with the murder.

Raymond Mercer's phone call actually helped out Floyd Zick as well. In such a case, it was natural to consider the husband as a potential suspect. Daisy was sleeping around on him. Perhaps Floyd had murdered his wife and had faked surprise when discovering her body. But the fact that Mercer made a phone call to her proved that Daisy was still alive after her husband had left the house. Furthermore the employees of Fales' Market all could account for his time during the morning. Just to be sure, Floyd Zick took a polygraph test and passed, indicating that he did not have any involvement in her murder.

The tension between the prosecutor and the state police did not abate. Besides complaining to the police that they had not included him immediately upon validating that a murder had taken place, Moore carried a chip on his shoulder in regard to the state police post commander in Battle Creek, Joe Svoke. The matter reached a head early in the investigation and got the Michigan State Police commissioner involved. His solution was eloquent. He ordered one of his top-notch detectives, Lieutenant Pat Detzler, to go to Battle Creek to smooth things over with Moore.

Patrick N. Detzler was close to retirement after a stellar career in the Michigan State Police. He had joined the force in 1937 and had served in Reed City, Rockwood and Center Line before making detective. Like most officers during the period, his occupation was one that called on him to constantly relocate to duty posts. During World War II, he had been exempt from service in the military but had served in a special investigation squad, a prestigious assignment during wartime. He was also one of a handful of state police troopers picked to act as a guard detail for President Harry Truman's visit to Michigan after the war. Later in life in 1948, he married Caroline Smith. They had two children.

Lieutenant Detzler was no slouch. He had earned two citations in his career. One was for a case in Paw Paw, Michigan, in which a man and his daughter had been swindled by a gypsy for $8,000 to have a hex removed from them. The second was for his work in a case where a teacher had been accused of sending an obscene letter. While there had been a rush to prosecute the teacher, Detzler had dug in and determined that the letter had actually been written by two high school students who were attempting to frame the teacher.

What Detzler brought to the Zick case was an air of professionalism and new perspective. His assignment seemed to calm Noble Moore, which made the cooperation between the state police and the prosecutor's office easier. One of his first actions was to integrate the investigators from the Calhoun County Sheriff's Department and the state police. Officers were paired up with one another, one from each department. This would provide complete transparency and demonstrate a willingness to work together. The two lead investigators were identified as Detective Charlie Conn and Undersheriff Wayne Fitch.

Prosecutor Noble Moore still felt that Audrey Heminger knew more than she was telling police. According to two sources, rumors had reached officers that Audrey and Daisy were involved in some sort of competition tied to the men they were allegedly sleeping with at the plant. To authorities, it seemed possible that Audrey may have been involved with the crime.

Three days after the murder, Moore had Audrey picked up by police at Kellogg's and brought to the state police post for a more intensive interview. The sudden pick up and the interview being done at the police post were techniques to intimidate a suspect and put him on unfamiliar ground. Detective Conn and Lieutenant Detzler were present, along with a court recorder. While Audrey was there of her own consent, the interview went badly. Moore was convinced that Audrey knew more and drilled her heavily about Daisy. She became so infuriated with the abrasive questions that she charged out. Ralph Kartheu, who was in the hallway at the time, recalled the event: "You could hear Moore's voice, it was pretty loud. Audrey came running out of the room crying. She ran down the steps and out the front door of the post. It was dark, she didn't have a car or anything, she just took off." Her cooperation in the case came to an abrupt end as the result of Moore's zeal. At the same time, she had managed to get out of the rest of the interrogation.

Almost a week after the murder, a pair of state troopers was dispatched down to Elkhart, Indiana, to locate Neville King, Daisy's first husband. Since 1944, he had been living in Elkhart, working at the Excel Company. King had heard of the murder when someone from Battle Creek had sent him an article on the killing. Neville was very cooperative with the troopers. According to him, Daisy was "noted to visit various male suspects." He also said that "the victim liked to <u>live it up</u>." The troopers confirmed that King was at work the entire day of the crime and was not likely to have been involved given that his contact with Daisy had diminished to nothing more than paying child support. The only person who had threatened to kill Daisy had an airtight alibi.

A rumor began circulating that Daisy had been raped in 1937, allegedly on government property. A check of the records did not reveal such a crime. The rumor does, however, correspond closely to a legal issue her ex-husband was embroiled with. In 1940, King had been involved with an assault on one Octavia Reese. The woman in question was under fifteen years of age, and King, who apparently had a penchant for younger women, had intercourse with the girl. Octavia became pregnant but miscarried, and despite the fact that King had expressed a desire to marry her, he ended up claiming that some other man was the father of the child. The court disagreed, though it admitted that the lack of control that Reese's mother had exhibited was a contributing factor to her situation. King spent time in Jackson State Penitentiary for six months for his crime. It is most likely that someone confused the crime involving King, and it became a rumor of rape involving Daisy.

Turning the focus on the employees of Kellogg's seemed logical for the investigators. Initially they looked at Daisy's rather wide circle of co-workers and friends at the factory. That was expanded to include anyone who missed work or couldn't be accounted for the day of the murder.

Kellogg's, like any large company, had a culture all its own. When you have thousands of people working closely, you are bound to have a number of people that have affairs. Male employees sometimes referred to their romantic partners as "shop wives," though they may have been married outside of work as well. Romances at Kellogg's didn't necessarily take place on the factory floor. Many people were discreet, only occasionally holding hands in front of co-workers. On the other hand, lunchtime trysts in the parking lot were not entirely uncommon. The couples that did this would often park next to each other each day. Others would leave the plant and either go home or to any number of known parking places for a quick fling. Those that couldn't wait could always find an isolated spot in the plant. As one person said, "My first day at Kellogg's, I got out of my car and saw a used condom in the parking lot. That seemed to say it all."

The night shift tended to be less stringent with the rules. As one summer employee working in the 1960s said, "The day shift was on the straight and narrow, but the night shift was like an ongoing party in the packing rooms. Couples would be playing music and dancing. It was bizarre." Alcohol was brought in to liven things up. In that kind of environment, Daisy's alleged promiscuity could only flourish.

Not everyone at Kellogg's was embroiled in such activities; in fact, the vast majority of employees just showed up and did their jobs. As Dorothy Kajcienski, a former co-worker of Daisy's, put it, "This kind of behavior wasn't prevalent. A lot of the female workers at the plant came from countries like Croatia and were good, hard-working people who concentrated on doing a good job." Dick Stevens of the prosecutor's office at the time had previously worked at Kellogg's with Daisy. "She worked in a fishbowl. It would have been impossible for her to carry on anything while on the line."

But Daisy did draw attention working out in the open. As Mrs. Kajcienski stated, "Daisy did turn heads…most people took a second look at her. She was a sharp dresser. She also wore makeup in the plant; that was something that most women didn't do."

Her reputation at Kellogg's was mixed, depending on whom you spoke to. Most spoke of her flirtatious attitude toward men, which fed many of

Daisy, *left*, with co-workers at the Kellogg's plant, 1940s. *Courtesy of James King.*

the rumors that she was fooling around with a number of men at the plant. Others, like Lynnette Rich, remember a warm and compassionate person who cared deeply about her fellow workers: "I remember that Daisy was the person who took a card around and collected money for my mother who had been in Ann Arbor for cobalt radiation treatment for cancer."

The police sweep of Kellogg's started with those individuals who knew Daisy. Some were off sick, such as Thomas Hurst, who was still in bed ill with the flu when the police located him. Others were ruled out because their timecards showed that they were still at work during the murder, but even they were asked to provide fingerprint samples to check against the unidentified latent print found in Daisy's car.

The police reports of these discussions indicate that some of the people at Kellogg's suffered from personal issues. One was a person excused because of his nervous breakdown and heavy drinking. Another had been fired from Kellogg's a week before the crime. According to his mother, he been home drunk on January 14 and was still drunk on the twenty-first, when the police called on him. One subject was known as a womanizer in the plant and was known to hit on numerous employees. His time was accounted for on the day of the murder, but like everyone else, he provided fingerprint samples.

The search of Daisy's locker spawned a number of rumors as well within the plant. The notes between her and Raymond Mercer leaked out somehow and grew as the story was retold. It evolved to be one in which the police had uncovered letters from a number of Daisy's lovers, all from Kellogg's, including some senior managers at the company. As time passed, these rumors took on more substance than reality.

The check of employees that were unaccounted for on the day and at the time of the crime netted nothing of use for the investigators. So they cast their search wider, pulling in any former Kellogg's employees who had left recently that might have known the victim. The ex-employees were a mix of individuals. One had been let for excessive drinking but had been cleared by witnesses at his new job. Others had simply taken other jobs and were surprised by the sudden appearance of police asking questions about the Zick murder.

The interrogation of Kellogg's employees was far from over. Daisy's co-workers on the line were interrogated next. Most, like Charles King, Eddie Lewis and Richard Darlington, knew Daisy but had no information of use. As many of the people at Kellogg's did, they proactively offered to take polygraph tests if it would help the police. Jack Motley, who had had a fender-bender with Daisy at the Kellogg's parking lot a year earlier, suddenly found himself being visited by police. Loretta Wierenga was cleared by witnesses that saw her paying her bills at the time of the crime. Her only connection to Daisy was that the two of them were part of a birthday club with Audrey Heminger and others at the plant. The investigators' zeal brought many people under suspicion.

The police expanded their search even further at the factory to look at anyone who fit the general description of the potential suspect provided by Mrs. DeFrance. This included people on other shifts who, in many cases, didn't even know Daisy. Investigators brought in a total of eighty-seven men from the line at the plant, asked for their alibis and fingerprinted and palm-printed them as a result of the sweep. Those that closely matched the physical description, as well as their friends, co-workers and wives, were contacted to validate the employees' whereabouts on January 14.

The effects of the investigation's focus on Kellogg's were staggering. Many people told me, off the record, that "Daisy's death broke up a lot of marriages." Certainly the police's probing at Kellogg's was the foundation of accusations of infidelity. While impossible to track, it is possible to imagine that spouses contacted to verify their husbands' connections, if any, to a murdered woman with a reputation for dating around would cause trouble for many innocent men. In all fairness, in numerous interviews, not a single couple was ever offered as an example of a marriage that ended because of Daisy's murder. It is most likely that these alleged shattered marriages are the stuff of urban legend tied to the Zick murder.

After three months' worth of digging into the workers at Kellogg's, the investigators still lacked anything useful to work with. All they had succeeded in doing was fuel the rumor mill at the factory. They continued to pursue other avenues of investigation. Two former boyfriends of Daisy were contacted, but both had solid alibis that ruled them out. A tip came in regarding a man that Daisy had been seen dancing with at the CIO Club, a bar in Battle Creek. A waitress at another bar, the Blinkerlite, reported that Daisy had frequented the establishment and that she and a man had been seen there twice in January prior to her murder. These leads turned out to be dead-ends as well. While they supported the theory that Daisy did date around and get out quite a bit, they did not help provide investigators with any information that could help the investigation.

Checks were made of criminals that were on parole for violent crimes, but Calhoun County had a remarkably small list of these. As these individuals were tracked down, each was found to have an alibi. Rapists were checked, though there had been no sign of sexual attack on Daisy. Also checked were individuals who had burglary charges, though there was little to indicate that Daisy had been killed as the result of a robbery. The lack of useful leads had forced police to search out even the improbable.

The Battle Creek Veterans' Hospital at Fort Custer became a focus for potential suspects. It was a common practice with law enforcement at the time given the number of mental patients housed there. Daisy's murder was so violent, the thinking was that it could potentially be the work of a mentally unstable person. The veterans' hospital's population of mental patients was sometimes released on passes. Historically, some patients on leave had contributed to Battle Creek's criminal activities, though nothing as horrific as Daisy's murder. Still, at the time, it seemed a viable line of investigation.

There were thirty-four patients on leave from the Veterans' Hospital who had not checked in by January 14. Most of the men unaccounted for were spread out all over the state. Thirteen different state police posts were enlisted to track them down. The effort to find them and validate their alibis consumed a massive number of hours. A handful of these men gave nonexistent addresses of where they were going while others were found to be on drinking binges while away from the hospital. Two were at YMCAs in different towns, and one was on a bus when the murder took place. Four men had left Battle Creek to go home and then checked into other veterans' hospitals in the state. The vast majority could not validate their activities but were clearly out of town at the time of the murder. Few of these men had heard of the crime, let alone the victim. Ultimately, these leads proved to be fruitless but required manpower to confirm.

The Kimball Sanatorium was checked to see if any of its male patients were unaccounted for at the time of the crime. There were eleven patients on the first floor that might have been considered, but all were accounted for. It was difficult to leave the sanatorium during the daytime hours and return undetected. While during the summer months the patients were allowed to walk the hospital grounds, in the winter, most were confined.

The police visited the Kalamazoo State Hospital, a mental care facility, on a tip that one of its patients, Alice Dodd, was claiming that she had killed Daisy. When the police arrived, however, they discovered a woman who was incapable of committing such a crime due to her mental state.

Other people turned in former spouses. Some of these men were unsavory at best. One man's former wife turned him in because he bowled at Ken Notke's Bowling Alley, which Daisy was known to frequent. He was an abusive man who had worked at Kellogg's and was known for his "deviant sexual activities," according to the ex-wife. This man was found to be living with his stepniece, now his wife, with a solid alibi.

In late January, Raymond Mercer came back to the forefront in the investigators' minds when a tip came in about a woman named Minnie Smith whom he was said to be having an affair with. Minnie and her husband lived next door to him at Long Lake in the 1950s. On top of that, she worked at Kellogg's with Mercer. Minnie had left Michigan to move to Florida two days after the murder. The day of the murder, she had come into the Kellogg Federal Credit Union and withdrawn all her money. That attracted the attention, as it appeared Minnie was leaving the state to flee from investigators.

Mercer's affair with Minnie lasted from 1955 to 1959. Investigators questioned him as to whether his wife had ever assaulted Minnie, to which Raymond responded that he was unaware of any such incident. They then looked into whether Minnie was a jealous former lover who wanted Daisy out of the way. Minnie indicated that she was long over Raymond Mercer by the time of Daisy's death and didn't know who Daisy Zick was. Furthermore, the time of day when Minnie withdrew her money roughly corresponded with the time that the murder took place. Minnie Smith proved to be another disappointing lead to Detzler's team.

An unnamed couple stopped by the *Battle Creek Enquirer and News* a few days after the murder and dropped off a check to start a reward offering for the crime. The newspaper deposited the money in an account called the Daisy Zick Reward Fund and invited local citizens to contribute. The money would be paid for any tip that led the prosecution and conviction to the murderer. Noble Moore and the state police would make the determination as to the distribution of the funds. Despite the plug in the paper, the fund never gained momentum.

A week after the death of his wife, Floyd Zick reached out to the investigators. He had received four phone calls at his home. On the other end was nothing but heavy breathing. He made arrangements to have his phone number changed to a new unlisted number. These were not the first phone calls of this type that he and Daisy had received. They had been getting what he thought were prank calls for the better part of the last year. The calls would come on Saturdays when Daisy was at home, and whoever it was would even call Floyd at Fales' Market. It sounded as if someone was talking through a piece of cloth to muffle his voice. In the era before caller ID, the phone company could not provide details on local calls. After Daisy's murder, these seemingly innocent calls took on new importance.

Floyd wasn't the only person who got mysterious calls. Mrs. DeFrance, whose name had been plastered in the newspapers as the eyewitness who saw the killer, started getting phone calls in January as well. She and her son, Jon, received calls from a female who simply stated, "A woman killed Daisy."

Chapter 5
NEW HOPES

I knew something was wrong—the kitchen rug was wadded up against the sink.
Floyd Zick
Battle Creek Enquirer and News
January 15, 1963

W e've all become a bit misled about how police investigations work thanks to movies and television. In our era of CSI and DNA, we've been shown that lab technicians solve most crimes by providing physical evidence to link the killer the crime. That is the Hollywood version of how it's done.

In the 1960s, and even today, a great deal of work was done by interviewing people, paying close attention to details, sharing information and following the directions of logical thinking. Evidence plays an important role, but many crimes are prosecuted every year on circumstantial evidence rather than something a lab tech has found.

The investigators of the Zick murder relied on this kind of police work to attempt to solve the crime. One of the early leads that came to investigators came in from observation. This particular lead began a few months before the murder. Fred Ritchie of the sheriff's department had been visiting with John Blodgett, the owner of the CIO Club in Battle Creek. The bar was frequented by the shifts coming off work from Post and Kellogg's. Ritchie, who was single at the time, was sitting in the car chatting with Blodgett, when they noticed an attractive redhead walking by.

The thirty-seven-year-old Blodgett made the comment that while the woman they were watching was attractive, he knew of another redhead that frequented his establishment. While he didn't name her, he gave tantalizing clues that stuck in Ritchie's head. She was from Wattles Park and was married. Furthermore, she was an employee at Kellogg's. According to Ritchie, Blodgett described her as "a wild one." At the time, the deputy gave it very little thought; it was simply the idle chatter of two men.

Unbeknownst to Fred Ritchie, the day after the murder, Wayne Fitch had stopped at the Mar Creek Inn in Ceresco, Michigan, about four miles from the Zick home. Fitch saw John Blodgett coming out of the bar, his clothing disheveled and a nasty cut on his face as if he had been scratched. It was obvious from what Fitch said he saw that Blodgett had been in some sort of fight. When he pressed the man as to what had happened to him, Mr. Blodgett answered that someone had told him a funny joke and he had fallen off of his bar stool. It seemed unlikely, but there was no reason to think differently.

The two officers, both working the case, brought up John Blodgett and compared notes. Was it possible that Daisy hung out at the CIO Club and that Blodgett had been involved with her?

A check of the tips that had come into the investigators certainly added some substance to their suspicion. Tip 122 was that Robert Allen of Marshall had been seen dancing with Daisy at the CIO Club a month or so before her murder. Police found that Allen worked at Kellogg's. In their check of Kellogg's, investigators validated his alibi. While Mr. Allen had proven to be a dead-end, this inquiry did place Daisy at the CIO Club.

The investigators turned their focus on Mr. Blodgett, eventually bringing him in for questioning and fingerprints. They even went so far as to propose that Blodgett take a polygraph examination. He agreed to do so and passed. His fingerprints did not match those recovered from Daisy's car either. While at first John Blodgett appeared to be a promising person of interest, he quickly became yet another painful dead-end for the investigation team.

As the winter slowly crept to an end, Lieutenant Detzler's team found itself floundering in a sea of dead-ends, pointless leads and other failed tips. The strategy of concentrating on Kellogg's that had seemed so promising back in January had done little more than cause marital strife with some of the employees who had been questioned.

The difficulty of pinpointing a suspect was uncommon in Calhoun County murders. Only two remained unsolved in the history of the county. Most killings were resolved relatively quickly, but after Daisy's death, the methods police had used to solve these cases were all used up with nothing to show. They opted to reach out to the public.

On February 2, two weeks after the murder, Prosecutor Moore assembled the investigative team along with the reporters from the local newspapers. The *Battle Creek Enquirer and News* intently covered the conference since the crime was still the talk of the town. The purpose of the meeting was to try to convince the public that they were indeed working hard on the case, while at the same time hopefully generate some new leads for the investigators. What unfolded was a candid discussion of some of the details of the case in hopes that the public would respond to them. Unfortunately, the press conference created more questions than answers.

"The murderer either walked or was driven to or near the Zick house," Moore told the press. He continued:

> *Either way he must have been seen. If he walked away after abandoning the Zick car, someone must have seen him and perhaps can give us a better description or can tell us in what direction he headed. If someone was waiting to pick him up in the area where he abandoned the car, that person can solve the murder now. Perhaps the driver is afraid to come forward. But now is the time. He—or she—should realize that one who conceals information of [a] crime is guilty of the crime himself.*

Detective Detzler threw in one theory they were looking at—that the killer might not be from the Battle Creek area. "It is possible that the slayer may have hitched a ride with someone passing through the area, such as a traveling salesman or someone who was stopping in the area on business and left before learning of the slaying," said Detzler.

The investigators continued to voice their theories. Robbery did not appear to be the cause the crime. "It is unlikely that a robber would have been so vicious in his assault of a robbery victim," Moore said. In reference to the forty-five dollars stolen from Daisy's wallet, he commented that it was "more likely the theft was an afterthought or was a cover up."

The police centered on the concept that the savage assault had to have been a crime of passion: "The physical evidence would indicate that the crime was either a crime of passion—incited by intense anger at the victim—or was committed by a sadist."

Was it possible that Daisy knew who it was that had come to kill her? According to the investigators, the service entrance door leading to the vestibule between the house and the garage was not locked and was the door that the man Mrs. DeFrance saw was standing at. Because the kitchen door was always locked, police had ruled it out as the point of entry, but Moore offered another theory: "Mrs. Zick could not see who was at the kitchen door. Therefore she could either have opened it in response to a voice she recognized or merely opened it in response to a knock without inquiring as to the visitor's identity."

Lieutenant Detzler discussed the cut telephone cord for the newsmen: "The cutting of the telephone wire obviously took place before Mrs. Zick was fatally stabbed, as the slayer could see after he had stabbed her that there was little chance of her using the telephone. As to why the wire was cut, one guess is as good as another at this time—she tried to call for help or she started to telephone someone the slayer did not want her to talk to are just two possibilities."

They informed the press that they had one unidentified fingerprint that may or may not belong to the murderer. They also emphasized that Floyd Zick had been highly cooperative and had passed his polygraph test "with flying colors."

The media had some questions of their own. The police had never broadcast a warning to the Wattles Park or Battle Creek community that a murderer was loose in the vicinity. This lapse, the media was quick to point out, might have put people at risk but also could have restricted immediate tips coming in. Moore added, "No one now needs to fear coming forward with information because he does not want to have his name publicized." He emphasized the point that the media might be excluded from information if it helped solve the case.

Moore ended the conference with a plea for assistance: "A person with any information has no way of knowing how important his or her fragment of information might be. It may be that with that information we already possess the fragment may complete an important segment on this jigsaw puzzle we are trying to put together."

———•—•———

There were other violent crimes in the region that the Michigan State Police were monitoring for similar circumstances. On February 5, 1963, a fifty-six-year-old female in Winona, Indiana, had been savagely attacked. Her assailant, an eighteen-year-old man, had stabbed her with her own butcher knife in the garage of her home. In Fort Wayne, Indiana, a month later, a white female was attacked by a twenty-two-year-old man with a steak knife. She was raped and then practically decapitated by her attacker. The Indiana State Police were able to ascertain that both of these killers had no connections to the area. Their names were not known by Floyd Zick as acquaintances of Daisy. Like so many hopeful tips, these quickly fizzled out.

Other jurisdictions with similar crimes that were unsolved reached out to the state police as well. From Culpeper, Virginia, the investigators of the double murder of Waltine Hoover and Annie Snow asked for copies of the case file and the crime scene photographs in hopes of finding some link to their crime. This too proved to be another dead-end.

In March, another crime in the western Michigan area seemed to offer a momentary glimmer of hope. Twenty-five-year-old Arthur Lee Jelks Jr. of Climax, Michigan, had been arrested for assaulting a woman. He had grabbed her and was attempting to drag her into his car when he was apprehended. Jelks was an employee of the Veterans' Hospital at Fort Custer. Violent crimes against women made a man a potential lead in the eyes of the investigators, and at first, Jelks seemed to be a candidate for questioning.

He claimed to know nothing about the Zick murder and agreed to a polygraph test. While he was clearly deceptive regarding the assault that he had been arrested for, Jelks appeared to know nothing about Daisy's killing, though he did confess to two purse snatchings in the area. His fingerprints and the polygraph cleared him as not having any involvement with Daisy's death. The investigators had to have been frustrated. But just as it seemed they were not making any progress, a new tip came in that changed everything. Someone had seen Daisy's murderer the day of the crime.

On March 23, 1963, the police got their first true break in the case in over two months. Forty-nine-year-old Garrettt Vander Meer contacted the state police to say that on the day of the murder he had gotten behind a white Pontiac on Michigan Avenue that had been driving slowly and erratically. When the car had come to a stop on the shoulder of the road near Evanston Street, he had finally gotten past it. Mr. Vander Meer stated that, as he had angrily passed the car, he got a good look at the driver. For the investigators, this was the first time that they got a good description of the man who had stolen Daisy's car.

Mr. Vander Meer had of course heard of the murder—it was the talk of Battle Creek. He had not immediately connected his encounter with Daisy's car to the event, however. His wife's friend Jane Millius had been talking about it when he started to draw the connection. When he pulled out the newspaper from that day, he recognized the photograph of Daisy:

> *That woman's picture, that got me too because at that grocery store at the corner of Wattles Park, they sell baked goods, Cummings Bakery, I guess it is. I go in there sometimes and get baked goods and go over to Jane's house and have coffee and rolls and that woman* [Daisy] *was in that store and that happened about a week before I saw her in there for the first time; but with that picture in the paper, I tumbled right away. After I found out about the car being at the top of the hill by Rose's house. That's when I tumbled. That's when I tumbled that that must have been the same car giving me a bad time at the bottom of the hill, and that's where it stopped.*

A chance encounter with Daisy at the Wattles Park Grocery had spurred the most critical tip the investigators had received since the first week of the investigation.

Detective Conn first took Vander Meer to the police garage where Daisy's car was still parked. Vander Meer confirmed it was indeed the same car he had seen. He was immediately brought in with a stenographer to meet with Detective Conn and several other officers.

Vander Meer had dropped off his wife to visit with a friend earlier that day and was on his way back to pick her up the morning of the murder. As best he could tell, it was just before or after 11:00 a.m. that morning. He had come up behind the Zicks' white Pontiac on Michigan Avenue just after the Wattles Road intersection near Hoff's Electrical: "I thought it was going to turn off the road and then go down there where that little side street is. Well, he didn't do that. He stayed on the edge of the pavement with his wheels still going on, going too slow, just like he was up to something, then he kept going, and I wondered if he was ever going to pull off or turn. Then when he got to where I thought he was going to turn, he didn't turn. He pulled off and stayed on the side of the road."

He estimated that the car was going ten to fifteen miles per hour and remembered that cars were beginning to line up behind Vander Meer's own car. He had to downshift his car because of the slow speed. With the rush of oncoming traffic, he couldn't pass the Pontiac until it finally pulled off the road. Vander Meer recalled: "His actions were definitely like he was looking for something, and he was looking out of his rearview mirror. But he wasn't glancing at any houses of anything. When a person looks for a house number, you know how they do [it]. You can spot them right away. He wasn't looking at house numbers, he was looking at something else."

As Vander Meer passed the car, he glared over at the driver that had been holding him up, and the two men made eye contact: "My car and his car weren't over six foot apart, and I stared at him and he stared at me; and I saw his face right then. Yes, I know what kind of hair he had and what he looked like, I know. He had some dark jacket on, dark blue I'd say, didn't look like black."

The police were very interested in every detail that Vander Meer could provide about the driver. The coat, they learned, was a thick winter jacket, similar to a navy peacoat. It had a zipper on the front that was pulled part of the way down. He wasn't sure about the shirt underneath other than that he knew that it wasn't white.

In terms of the driver, "I'd say he was a good sized fellow, and a good looking man. He wasn't homely, and he was bare headed, didn't have no cigarette in his mouth and was staring right at me, and I was giving it to him because there were cars behind me too, and he slowed us all down."

When pressed for further details, Vander Meer was able to provide them: "He had a bit of color in his face. It was white, it wasn't real red. Kinda medium-sized face." He went on to describe to them a driver who was clean shaven and "healthy looking." When asked to describe the nose of the man, "Well, that doggone nose—it wasn't a fat nose, I know that. It was more on the slim side." He added, "It wasn't a skinny face, no. It wasn't puffed up like some of them people have got—puffed up cheeks. It wasn't like that."

Vander Meer described him as a man roughly his own size—five foot eleven—based on him sitting in Daisy's car. He was slim in build. He guessed the age of the driver as thirty to thirty-five years old.

The most distinctive feature the man had was his hairstyle. It was raised in the front and combed back. Rather than being sleeked back, it puffed up in the front. The hair was "combed straight back in the parts. Would have had maybe a slight wave but not real deep." From his accounts the man's hair was not black, but a dark brown.

Detective Conn pressed for every possible detail. Did Vander Meer see the driver's hand on the steering wheel by any chance? "When he was over the side of the road he had his hand on the steering wheel, I know that, but his hand looked like a normal hand, didn't look like a fat hand." He didn't have any gloves on.

Vander Meer worked with the officers to develop a composite drawing of the man that was behind the wheel of Daisy's Pontiac. The police used an Identi-Kit to attempt to recreate the driver's face. This was a set of transparencies with various facial characteristics that could be laid on top of each other to form a composite image of the driver. The only issue with the Identi-Kit was that it did not have the hairstyle that Mr. Vander Meer saw on the man.

In terms of other cars alongside the road, Vander Meer replied, "All I remember was, I think, a foreign car in the snow in front of that greenhouse, looked like it had been sitting there a long time, lots of snow under it. And then up on the hill a little ways I thought there was a car there but I am not positive what it was." He added that he did not see anyone walking on Michigan Avenue that day.

He was sure that he could identify the man again if he saw him. When asked if he would be willing to attempt to identify the driver, Vander Meer said he would be glad to try. Having a witness that could potentially identify the murderer was useful but didn't help the police locate the suspect for identification. The police were divided as to where to focus the search for Daisy's killer.

Kellogg's, which had been such a promising area of concentration in the investigation, had proven to be a bust so far. While police had a good witness who could identify the killer, they did not release this information to the press, nor did they put out the artist's image of what the murderer looked like. Vander Meer's contribution to the case was kept quiet, as is common in such instances, so as to not tip off the perpetrator. They held out hope that he would one day be able to identify the killer in a court of law. For them, it was a proverbial ace up the sleeve.

———•◦•———

The first big setback in the investigation came in an unlikely form. On May 7, 1963, Undersheriff Wayne Fitch was doing his weekly work mowing the lawn at the First Presbyterian Church in Marshall. It was a warm day, proof that spring was finally settling into the region. He had been working long hours since January almost exclusively on the Daisy Zick case. As he pushed the power mower, Wayne Fitch suffered a heart attack.

Wayne managed to call for help, and the Kelser Ambulance Service a block away got him to the hospital. The trip to Oaklawn Hospital in Marshall was only a matter of minutes, but despite the fast response and the proximity of medical help, Wayne Fitch passed away less than an hour after his arrival.

His funeral service was one of the largest in Marshall that year. Police officers from countless jurisdictions attended, not out of obligation but respect. In his job, Wayne Fitch touched a lot of people's lives, from testing students for their driver's licenses to his swift and fair administration of his sworn duties. Fitch was an icon of the community. Sheriff Jess Purcell said, "He has been a very good officer. His loss will be deeply felt by our department and law enforcement departments in this part of Michigan. He was not only a good officer, but a good friend." Sheriff Purcell's comments were echoed by other police chiefs in the county.

The truth of the matter was that Daisy's murderer had taken another life, albeit indirectly. Fitch's role in the investigation was to be filled by Captain Billie O. Patterson, a competent officer in his own right. Patterson was a big man but with a soft-spoken voice. He had been working on the case as needed, but after Fitch's death, he was pulled in to take the lead for the sheriff's department. Fitch's death was the first loss to the investigation team.

———•◦•———

The police still held out hope that the evidence might tie the perpetrator to the crime. One of the most compelling bits of evidence was the yellow fibers recovered at the murder scene. These yellow cotton fibers were believed to be from work or hunting gloves, but so far, the state crime lab had not been able to match the fibers to any particular model or type of glove on the market. Still, they were a potential link to the killer.

When Gilbert Sullivan broke out of the Michigan Reformatory in Ionia, the police searched a house owned or rented by Patrick Densmore looking for their man. The Battle Creek Police Department search took them into every nook and cranny of the home. In the stuffy hot attic of the home, the city police came across a stained yellow work glove, with hair trapped in its fibers. Additional searching produced a white lady's glove covered with a brown or yellowish substance. Since the home was in Battle Creek, the officers were well aware of the Zick case. The prosecutor's office and the state police were informed of the find and issued a warrant to the search for evidence related to Daisy's murder. Meanwhile, the officers put the gloves in a bag, and within an hour, they were in the possession of Detective Conn. He turned them over to the Michigan State Department of Health laboratory for analysis and logged them as Tip 198 in the voluminous Daisy Zick case file. The hope was that the fibers of the glove might be identical to those recovered at the crime scene.

It took a few days for the result to come back, and with it, more disappointing news. The gloves were not a match at all. The stains were not blood, and the hair that was recovered proved to be from an animal. It was another disappointing dead-end. Tip 198 proved to be no more revealing than its 197 predecessors.

Another lead came in from neighboring Kalamazoo, where Vernon Bowers was under arrest for murder. He was a parolee living with his common-law wife, Averill "Bucky" Cropp, who was a female entertainer in the county. They had been living in the El Rancho Trailer Park, when Bowers had strangled Cropp using a wire coat-hanger. There was little question as to his guilt. Bowers had said that his murder of Cropp had been a "mercy killing."

Bower's arrest record caught the attention of the Zick investigators. He had been arrested for larceny, indecent liberties, entering without breaking in and grand larceny. The police met with him to ascertain any possible connection with Daisy.

According to Bowers, he didn't know Daisy Zick other than from reading about the murder in the local paper. His alibi was thin, as he said that he was most likely at home with Cropp, the woman he murdered, on the night of the crime. The officers took a copy of his fingerprints and checked them against the print in the Zick Pontiac, and there was no match. Given the lack of connection between Bowers and Daisy, the police ruled him out as a potential suspect.

After the Sullivan and Bowers leads in the case began to dry up, it seemed as if every potential avenue that the police checked into led them nowhere. And then the case suffered its next major loss on the investigation team: on Halloween 1963, Lieutenant Patrick N. Detzler retired from the Michigan State Police.

Lieutenant Detzler had been sent to Battle Creek to perform two duties. One was to repair the relationship between local law enforcement (including the prosecutor's office) and the state police. The other was to assume the leadership in the Daisy Zick murder and bring that case to a conclusion. In his first task, Detzler had been successful. His pairing up of sheriff's department deputies with state police troopers and his cooperation with Noble Moore had gone a long way in smoothing over the damaged relationships.

His second role, however, remained incomplete. By October 1963, the leads in the Zick investigation had all but disintegrated. Troopers such as Ralph Kartheu had been told to put their uniforms back on and return to patrol duty. There simply weren't enough tips coming in to warrant keeping men on the case full time. Soon, the only men left to the case were Detective Conn and Captain Patterson.

Chapter 6

THE COLD SETS IN

It is still not too late for that person to come forward, to put aside the fear of what the killer might do or because he or she is afraid of becoming involved.
Detective Charlie Conn
One year after Daisy Zick's murder

One state police detective told me that some cases are allowed to go cold on purpose:

> *When a perpetrator knows that we are hot on their trail, they tend to clam up. Nervous criminals are more careful about what they say and to whom they speak. Sometimes we allow a case to go cold so that a criminal will relax. He or she will start to talk to others, get lax in his behaviors. When they relax they share secrets with others that helps us sometimes fill in the missing gaps on an investigation. They have a slip of the tongue about their crime, then a jilted friend or lover comes forward and talks. Allowing a case to go cold sometimes can really help us with an investigation.*

This was not the case with Daisy Zick's murder. Her case went cold because every lead seemed to evaporate. There was hope that, as the citizens of Battle Creek relaxed, someone would come forward with new information, but that simply didn't happen.

There were other reasons the investigation had stalled as well. The investigation team had focused on the motive as the pathway to finding the

Daisy in the 1950s with Bubbles, their dog. *Courtesy of James King.*

murderer. In reality, however, they had not agreed among themselves as to what the motive of the killer was. This meant that each investigator had his own theory as to who might have committed the crime and why.

Detective Conn believed that the killer had to be a psychopath to have been so brutal. He favored the young hitchhiker, though the man had already been cleared in the investigation. The man had several crimes involving women under his belt and was known to be strange for collecting newspapers. He had been seen hitchhiking in the area the day of the crime, though that tip had come from the person that had claimed he had seen two men driving away from Daisy's car—an admitted lie. Despite the fact that he had been cleared by both polygraph and by fingerprints, Conn felt that his mental state might have allowed him to falsely pass the polygraph.

As Ralph Kartheu put it, "You can't beat the polygraph, but you can beat the operator." The physical reactions to lies are difficult to conceal, but operators do make mistakes. As another detective, Gary Hough, on the case years later, said, "Sometimes it's as subtle as the wording of a question that allows someone to slide by. The skill of the operator is what makes it a useful tool."

Others felt that the savage nature of the murder clearly pointed to someone who had an existing relationship with Daisy. Their logic was that this appeared to be a crime of passion and that only someone who had an intimate relationship with Daisy would have been so brutal in his implementation of the crime. This had dominated the thinking of the investigators and had led to the detailed probe of the workers at Kellogg's and the attempts to track down the men that Daisy may or may not have had relationships with.

Others on the investigation team, such as Ralph Kartheu, felt that the killer wasn't a man at all:

> *Months before the crime I had attended an FBI training course up in Lansing. It was about profiling killers. When I saw the wounds on Daisy, I remembered that training, and it struck me that the murderer was likely a woman. The attacks on Daisy in the guest bedroom were almost all on her left breast. Women often do that kind of brutality against another woman. It is a way to attack the sex of the victim.*

In Kartheu's mind, the killer was a woman; perhaps the spouse of someone that Daisy was having an affair with. Criminal profiling was in its infancy in the 1960s, but there was some good logic behind Kartheu's thinking: "One of the problems I had was that the other investigators had a hard time thinking that a woman could be so vicious. In the 1960s, you just didn't have a lot of woman murderers—not like this."

Not many female suspects had been considered. The only one brought in directly for interrogation was Audrey Heminger, and she had stormed out of her interview session. While it was possible that a jealous wife had come after Daisy, it seemed unlikely that she would have opened the door for such a confrontation when preparing to leave for her lunch appointment.

With each investigator looking for someone fitting his own mental picture of the killer, the investigation lacked continuity. The team really didn't have much of a choice but to follow their instincts on motive in the hope that they would lead them to a suspect. The other option was to follow the crime scene evidence, and in this case, it was relatively thin for 1963 standards.

The evidence still retained by the Michigan State Police numbers thirty items, each meticulously maintained to this day. The recovered evidence includes:

Hairs and fiber from the victim's pants and slacks.
Known fibers from the carpet in the bathroom and hall.
Hairs and fibers recovered from the bedspread.
Scrapings of blood from the footboard of the bed.
Fibers and hairs from the victim's blouse.
Hair recovered from Daisy's vanity stool.
Green fibers from a plaid skirt.

Blue fibers from slacks found in the southwest bedroom closet.
Red fibers from the trousers of Floyd Zick.
The victim's blouse, brassiere, shoes, slacks and panties.
Blood and hair samples taken from the victim.
Yellow fibers recovered from behind the victim's right ear.
The bathrobe sash used to tie her hands.
The white bedspread.
Yellow fibers recovered from the garage door.
Scrapings (presumed to be blood) taken from the kitchen sink.
Scrapings from the door handle of Daisy's Pontiac.
A terry-cloth towel from the kitchen.
Hair samples from Floyd Zick.
A pair of cotton work gloves.
Fibers recovered from the bumper of Daisy's Pontiac.
Fibers recovered from inside of Daisy's show boots.
Daisy's handbag and contents (her checkbook, billfold and papers, two one-dollar bills, one half-dollar coin, three nickels and two pennies).
A jackknife recovered from the Zick home.
One cotton glove.
One cloth bag.
The Spoilage knife believed by some to be the murder weapon.
One white button.
Two pieces of telephone cord taken from either side where it was severed by the killer.
Photographs and negatives of the fabric impression on the car.

The evidence told a story in 1963, but at best, it was a jigsaw puzzle in which the assembled image was unknown. In an age before DNA testing, Daisy's bloody clothing could only be tested for the blood type and verify if it was human. The Spoilage knife recovered from the Zick home could not be verified as the murder weapon. There was a button recovered from the floor of the Zick bedroom that was not Daisy's or Frank's, making it most likely the murderer's, but that assumption was impossible to prove without the garment that it was from.

That only left the fiber and fingerprint evidence recovered from Daisy, the crime scene and her car. The evidence, while tangible, did not steer investigators in any one direction or toward a potential suspect. It simply stood mute, waiting for a time when it could see its day in court. Unfortunately, that day still has not come.

On the one-year anniversary of the crime, Prosecutor Moore tried to stir up tips from the public. By 1964, the world had changed. Meat prices had "soared" to thirty-nine cents a pound. The Bijou Theatre in Battle Creek was playing *The Prize*, and the top song in the country was Bobby Vinton's "There I've Said it Again," followed shortly by one from a new group, the Beatles' "I Want to Hold Your Hand."

This time, Moore went in two different directions. The first was in the form of an article in the *Battle Creek Enquirer and News*. The second was an interview on the case in *True Detective* magazine.

The decision to turn to *True Detective* was not unprecedented but was a stretch. The entire genre of the early pulp magazines dedicated to true crime was one that was a bit seedy but, at the same time, had great potential reach. The genre had been born in 1924, when a number of the magazines had emerged on the market, catering to detailing true crime tales complete with artwork and photos.

Originally the magazines focused on gangster-style crimes. Even the legendary J. Edgar Hoover was said to be a fan of the magazines, as were many in law enforcement. The magazines sensationalized criminal cases and the officers who cracked them, and for some law officers, it was a way to get national exposure for what might be a local crime. What made the magazines of this genre stand out at first were the graphic images of victims that newspapers or other more reputable magazines rarely showed. Because of this sensationalism, there was an air of "adult content only" when it came to these magazines. Despite negative rap, at its peak, *True Detective* had over two million readers each month.

The people that wrote the articles for *True Detective* sometimes were law enforcement officers but usually were newspaper journalists. People that covered crimes in their local paper found that writing articles on the same crimes for *True Detective* allowed them to make significant money. They would even take photographs from the newspaper archives they worked for and used them in the articles. To avoid being caught and reprimanded, they often wrote under a pseudonym.

By the 1950s and '60s, the genre had started to devolve. The covers almost always had a female in either some sort of bondage pose or taking part in some crime either as a criminal or, more often, a victim. Oftentimes, the covers had little to nothing to do with the actual articles inside; they were images aimed simply at drawing attention. The May 1964 issue of

True Detective, which featured the article on the Daisy Zick murder, was no different. It featured a woman viewed through a keyhole, paralyzed with fear with a switchblade held to her throat.

In the newspaper interview, Moore drew out the thick folder that constituted the case file for the Zick murder. He, Detective Conn and Captain Patterson sat in his office and allowed the reporter to grill them. After a year of investigation, there had been a total of 243 tips and leads that had come in from the public, all of which had been investigated. The investigation team had interviewed over eight hundred people, with polygraphs given to over a dozen individuals. None of these had yielded a suspect for them to focus on. Whereas a dozen officers from the sheriff's department and the state police had been working the case in the beginning, only Conn and Patterson remained.

Moore and the investigators did not reveal everything they had in the case, such as Garrett Vander Meer's good visual of the driver of the car and the fiber evidence they had recovered. It was a fairly standard procedure in such a case to withhold information that would help them if a suspect was potentially identified. What they did emphasize was the fingerprint they still had not identified: "The print, the only one of several that was not identified by the state police fingerprint experts, was found on the inside of the car of Mrs. Zick; the car that the slayer drove from her garage and abandoned on East Michigan Avenue near Evanston Avenue, about a mile and a half from the Zick home." Conn also commented that whoever the killer was, he had taken Mrs. Zick's car keys with him.

Conn was candid with an admission that despite their hard work, the investigators had not settled on one theory regarding the killer: "Mrs. Zick, police say, was wary of admitting strangers to her home. The solid door leading from the garage into the Zick kitchen was usually locked. Did she open it to her murderer because she recognized a familiar voice, or did a stranger trick her into opening the door?"

One thing most investigators agreed on was that the ferocity of the assault pointed to someone who had a deep personal issue with Daisy. The crime was, "either a crime of passion—indicated by intense anger at the victim—or the act of a sadist."

Moore solidified that they had not given up on finding a killer: "The case is not marked 'closed' or even 'inactive.'"

The interview with *True Detective* included Noble Moore, Captain Patterson and Detective Conn as well. Its title was "Michigan's No. 1 Murder Mystery" and was a somber plea for help from the public. Moore summed up the investigation: "Except for having eliminated a great number of possible suspects, we are no closer to the solution of this case than we were a year ago.

"During those first weeks, a number of tips were received as a result of press, radio and TV interested in the case. We hope that by opening our files to *True Detective Magazine* someone, somewhere, might remember and provide us with new, important information."

Detective Conn was even more somber: "This case is unlike most murder cases. In most murder cases you discover a motive—robbery, sex, jealousy, fear. In this case any one of these could have been the motive."

When one looks at these motives compared to the evidence, they seem to be strained. Robbery didn't make sense. Daisy's purse was missing forty-five dollars, but its theft certainly didn't warrant the kind of brutality she suffered in her last minutes. There was no indication of rape except her pants' zipper being pulled down, though had her killer wanted to rape her, it certainly would have been possible, as her hands were tied behind her back.

Out of all of the motives considered, jealousy seemed to be the one that warranted the level of violence that had been committed. It could have been a former or current lover or a spouse of one of Daisy's suitors that had gone after her. "From the stories we have heard so far, Mrs. Zick was friendly and had a warm personality. If the slayer did know her, it could be someone that misinterpreted a smile or a friendly word. Also she might have been interested in some other man before her marriage to Zick in 1945, or after. We will have to try and find out if there might have been such a man, and who he was," Conn contributed.

It was possible fear had caused the extreme violence. The killer could have come to commit one crime and things had simply gotten out of hand, leading to murder. But that scenario seemed highly unlikely because of the extremes the killer went through to reach the Zick home—a sign of premeditation. One clue did seem to point to the spontaneity of the crime: the fact that the potential murder weapon, the Spoilage knife, was in the house. Other than that, the case did not appear to be a crime run amok.

The interview, similar to the newspaper article, focused on the one piece of evidence that the team felt could tie the killer to the crime: the unidentified fingerprint recovered from Daisy's Pontiac. "We believe it is the murderer's print," Moore stated.

The publication of the article in *True Detective* elevated the status of the Zick case. No longer was it simply about a murder in Battle Creek; it was now playing out on a national stage. Wayne Moore of Flint, Michigan, contacted the state police and said that he had read the article and that two of his young boys had recently found a set of keys. He remembered from the magazine article that the killer had taken Daisy's keys with him. Could these be those keys?

Floyd Zick had to be contacted for a description of what keys were on Daisy's ring. There were two sets of Pontiac keys (two each), a house key and one for her locker at Kellogg's. The six keys were on a split ring. The keys that Moore's boys found were ten total, ruling them out. Sadly, this was the biggest tip that came out of publication of the article.

Ultimately the article in *True Detective* had no great sway in the case other than to bring the story to a wider audience. Daisy's status as Michigan's number one murder mystery would continue for a few more years until other events superseded the crime.

The unfortunate turnout of tips wasn't to say that there weren't some tantalizing moments when the investigators thought they might have a break. A week before the first anniversary of the crime, Derwin J. Workman of Big Rapids, Michigan, had brutally killed his ex-wife in her apartment.

Workman was a troubled man. He and his wife had divorced eight months earlier. He claimed that she had promised that they could get back together. Derwin had secured a marriage license on January 6, 1963, the same day he killed his former spouse. When he had contacted his ex-wife, she told him that she had changed her mind.

It was too much for him.

Workman crashed through the front window of her apartment and went after his wife with a hunting knife, while his two small sons screamed in terror. He trapped his wife and savagely stabbed her eighteen times, mostly in the chest. Police apprehended him quickly and locked him away.

Apart from the brutality of the attack and the use of a knife, there didn't seem to be much that might tie Derwin Workman to Daisy's death. Detective Conn and Captain Patterson decided that it was worth checking into Workman's whereabouts a year earlier, if only to rule him out. What they found, however, was that Workman had been in Battle Creek in February 1963, two weeks after Daisy's murder. Suddenly, Workman became a momentary focus for the investigators.

Workman had been living in the Battle Creek area in February 1963. He had been committed to the veterans' hospital at Fort Custer in May after another incident in which he had attacked his wife with a knife in December 1962. A probate judge in Midland, Michigan, had ordered him committed to the hospital for treatment. It was a sentence that had eventually doomed Mrs. Workman to be killed as her children watched.

With so many links to the Battle Creek area and a propensity to favor a knife as a weapon, it appeared that Workman could potentially be linked to Daisy's death. But it was not meant to be. Records produced by Workman confirmed that in January 1963, at the time of Zick murder, he was back living with his wife in Big Rapids. Workman's fingerprints were submitted to the state police crime lab for comparison against the sole print recovered from the Zick's Pontiac. They were not a match. It became another disappointment in a long series faced by the investigators.

After the investigation into Workman, the leads slowed to an agonizing trickle. Only once a month did something come in that Detective Conn could even consider following up on. Most were vague dead-ends, such as the tip that came in on March 3, 1964. While stopped at a train crossing in Battle Creek (a common occurrence), a female driver was stunned when her male passenger (who owned the car) suddenly erupted in anger, kicking at the door and punching the window with his fists. As she talked to him, he assured her that he didn't want to kill her. At the same time, he mentioned a woman named "Zink" or something similar to that. The man kept on punching the window in frustration, talking about the woman, referring to her as a "bitch." The only identification provided beyond his age (thirty-eight to thirty-nine), his glasses and his light brown hair was that the man was named Jerry and he frequented the Idlehour and Verona taverns and Speeds Restaurant. She offered to contact the police when she saw Jerry again to point him out.

Another lead came from Detective Kolahmainen of the state police intelligence unit. He had read a newspaper article about the murder of a young woman in Chicago who had been viciously stabbed. Her killer was one Robert Engler, who had been captured in Uniontown, Pennsylvania. Detective Kolahmainen surmised that there might be a link between this stabbing and that of Daisy, a remarkable bit of thinking given that this was the era before the internet or even computers being used by police. The Uniontown police mailed a copy of his fingerprints in, and they were checked against the unidentified print found in Daisy's car, again with no results.

Such tips, even on the surface, would seem barely worth noting. They were the caliber of leads that the investigators were receiving, increasingly in painfully smaller numbers. The police took each one seriously though; they had to. The public fervor over Daisy's murder had not died down. Some of that was because of the invasive manner in which the tight-knit community at Kellogg's had been penetrated. Another aspect was the pure violent nature of her death and the fear that it brought the community.

—·•·—

The public scrutiny of Floyd Zick did not abate after his being cleared by the polygraph and having an airtight alibi for the crime. He tried to move on with his life as best he could. He frequented several bars and was known to take the microphone and sing for the audience if the mood was on him, though his voice was not nearly as good as he thought it was. People watched Floyd, some secretly believing that he knew more about his wife's death than he had let on.

Selling the home on Juno Street proved impossible with the local community so aware of the murder that had taken place there. Floyd remained in the house for several years.

Several sources have said that Floyd was an alcoholic prior to the murder but was a functional drinker. He was not tardy for work at Fales' Market and always was personable with customers. After the death of his wife, he had become more sullen and began to drink more heavily.

He remarried over a year after Daisy's death. His bride was Doris Epley, a waitress. Those that knew Floyd said he was overly protective of Doris, always keeping close tabs on her, no doubt a result of the events that had come to dominate his life.

As much as he tried to move on, it was clear that the death of Daisy weighed heavily on him. He gave her jewelry away. He eventually sold her car to Marie Fales as her first car. Her mother insisted that the car be repainted. This was, after all, the car that the killer had driven from the place of the murder in. The last thing Mrs. Fales wanted was her young daughter driving around in a car that might be recognized by the killer, who was still on the loose.

By March 1965, Floyd had become dependent on his drinking. He was committed to the Battle Creek Sanitarium for treatment. Detective Conn, upon hearing of this, used the opportunity to visit the new Mrs. Zick to probe to see if Floyd had ever revealed any information about the crime to her. Perhaps, just perhaps, Floyd was struggling with guilt over his first wife's death, or he may have remembered something that he had let slip to his new spouse. Doris Zick said that her husband had never discussed with her anything about Daisy nor given her any information that would lead her to believe that he was involved. Detective Conn and the investigators left Floyd alone as he recovered.

———•◦•———

By 1965, every lead was cold. Detective Conn and Captain Patterson were shifted to new cases, ones that stood a chance of being solved. The Zick files were carefully catalogued by Trooper Kartheu and boxed up. It had become painfully clear that the original investigators were not likely to be the ones to solve the crime. Indeed, both Fitch and Detzler were already gone. The public had trouble letting go of the Zick case—some because of the possible involvement of someone at Kellogg's, others out of fear that whoever committed such a heinous crime might strike again. The obligation to continue this investigation was about to fall to a new generation of investigators.

When I talked to Battle Creek law enforcement officers of the era, almost all said that one of the biggest changes to happen to the Michigan State Police Post Forty-six in the 1960s was the arrival of two officers: detectives

Detectives Kenney and Steinbacker. *Courtesy of Anita (Kenney) Stockham.*

Robert Kenney and Leroy Steinbacher. As Fred Ritchie put it, "Things really improved over there when Kenney and Steinbacher arrived. They were top-notch investigators, real professionals."

Robert Kenney was from Amasa in Michigan's Upper Peninsula. He had been rotated to a number of posts before coming to Battle Creek with his wife and children. At six foot two with crew cut "cop hair," he was a determined and methodical investigator.

Leroy Steinbacher—"Stein," as some called him—was a husky-built man with a square jaw and slicked-back hair. He had been raised in the Battle Creek area and was seven years Kenney's senior. Detective Steinbacher was known to be tenacious when he worked on a case, determined to see it through to its conclusion.

Kenney and Steinbacher were to be drawn into the Zick case starting in 1965. For one of them, it would be an obsession that continued long after he left the police force.

Chapter 7
A NEW GENERATION OF INVESTIGATORS

Retired Michigan State Police Detective Leroy Steinbacher says murder is the most violent act one person can commit against another. He still thinks about unsolved murders a quarter century after he retired. "If you are good you won't sleep at night," he said. "I want to get them and put them away so they won't do it again. And it is a deterrent for others. I was always working for the proper justice." Twenty-five years after his retirement and 35 years after the unsolved murder of a Battle Creek woman, Daisy Zick, Steinbacher still thinks about that case. He believes there is a chance the murder can still be solved and hates the thought that he might die before the killer is caught. "I would give anything to see someone convicted."

Battle Creek Enquirer and News
February 1, 1998

Detective Leroy Steinbacher first became involved with the murder of Daisy Zick in November 1965. An informant contacted Steinbacher and told him the name of a potential suspect, Roland Bouchard. According to the anonymous tip, Bouchard was charged with attempted rape and was known to have a violent temper. Bouchard was a bartender at the Chuck Wagon bar and restaurant in 1963 at the time of the murder and quit his job there shortly after Daisy's murder. The informant added that Bouchard had scratches on his face just after the crime.

For Steinbacher, or for any detective getting such a tip, this meant that he would have to sit down with the massive Zick file and review the information from the crime scene and the evidence to date. It would be a massive undertaking and an immersion in all of the investigation that had taken place prior to his involvement.

Bouchard had been arrested two times for breaking and entering prior to coming to the attention of the Zick investigators. He had spent three years in Jackson State Penitentiary and had been on parole for two years. In 1961, he had been brought up on charges of attempted rape. Bouchard had been arrested by the Owosso Police Department for disorderly conduct, a case which was still pending. While the informant's tip about attempted rape didn't hold water, one thing was for sure: Mr. Bouchard was no stranger to law enforcement. The judge in Owosso was reluctant to release Bouchard's fingerprints for testing to Detective Steinbacher. After all, Bouchard had been arrested for a misdemeanor, and the detective was looking into a murder case. He eventually relented.

The disorderly conduct charge had come from Bouchard allegedly calling women on the phone and using "obscene and immoral language" as well as making threats. One of the victims had the police tap her line, and the call was traced back to a local phone booth where witnesses recalled seeing Bouchard at the time.

The Chuck Wagon's proximity to where Daisy's car had been abandoned couldn't be ignored; it was only a half mile down the road, almost within eyesight of where the Pontiac had been left by the murderer. Even more intriguing was the fact that the current Mrs. Zick, Doris, was employed there as a barmaid.

Steinbacher went to the bar to interview the staff. Helen Greenfield recalled Bouchard as "a ladies' man." Another waitress there, Eve Jordon, had dated Bouchard for a short time, but Helen had felt that he was too young for Eve's interests.

The coincidence of Floyd Zick's new wife working at the same place as someone suggested as his first wife's murderer was enough for Detective Steinbacher to have Floyd come out to the state police post for questioning. The new prosecuting attorney, John Jereck, sat in on the session as did a sergeant from the post. Floyd Zick was very nervous and upset when he was questioned. He knew Bouchard as a driver for Farm Peets eight years earlier. After Daisy's death, Floyd had frequented the Chuck Wagon and had seen him as a bartender there, but that was the depth of their relationship.

Doris offered less to investigators. Yes, she worked at the Chuck Wagon, but she did not know of any relationship between Floyd and Bouchard. She described Floyd as being very upset since the time of their marriage.

Another man questioned was the part-time organist at the Chuck Wagon, Ralph Hartom. Hartom said that Bouchard was a well-known ladies' man and had a violent temper. When asked about Floyd Zick, Hartom replied that he did know him and described him as lonely since the death of Daisy and a heavy drinker. The short-statured Hartom, described in the police reports as a possible homosexual, had admitted that he was a friend of Floyd Zick and had even spent the night in the Zick home, though he said that he had not known Daisy prior to her death.

Roland Bouchard had been arrested in December 1965 on a maternity warrant from Van Buren County. At five feet seven inches tall and 136 pounds, Bouchard was a strong man who seemed to have ongoing issues with the law. When not under arrest, he was a brakeman for the Ann Arbor Railroad. Detective Steinbacher and Sergeant LaPointe both made arrangements to interview him.

Ever the seasoned policeman, Steinbacher did not jump in with questions about Daisy Zick. Instead he asked about Bouchard's past arrests, letting his subject relax. Then he raised the specter that Bouchard might be connected in some way to Daisy's murder, at which time "[Bouchard] became very disturbed and [it] was the opinion of the officers that he could be involved or have knowledge of the same." According to Bouchard, he only knew about the case from the newspapers and the article in the *True Detective* magazine. He admitted that he had spoken with Floyd Zick about the murder at the Chuck Wagon, but that was all. Still, his agitation drew the attention of Steinbacher. For the first time in a long time, it appeared there might be some sort of break in the case.

Roland Bouchard agreed to a polygraph test, and it was administered in the Paw Paw State Police Post. It appeared that Bouchard was not withholding information on the case. Still, polygraphs were not infallible. Despite his passing the test, Steinbacher had the state police crime lab test Roland Bouchard's fingerprints with the unidentified print lifted from Daisy's car. They were not a match. While this seemed to be a dead-end, this involvement in the case by Steinbacher marked the first step in his many years' journey on the Zick murder.

Roy Bechtol was the Emmett Township police chief in 1964 and had his own insights into the Zick murder. Bechtol was a Battle Creek native who started as a patrolman for the Battle Creek Township Police. He worked on the Civil Defense Reserve Force and had worked full time after that for the Calhoun County Sheriff's Department. He took a job with the fledgling Emmett Township Police Department in 1963 and, by 1964, had been named its chief. When the Zick murder had first occurred, he had been working closely with Undersheriff Wayne Fitch, so Bechtol was no stranger to the investigation.

In January 1964, Bechtol had received a tip that Albert Earl Cooley may have been romantically involved with Daisy Zick. On his own accord, he decided to question Cooley about his alleged relationship. Cooley didn't admit to an affair but did reveal that he had a girlfriend that lived on Eisenhower, right near the Dog 'n Suds within eyesight of where Daisy's car had been abandoned. "When I questioned him, he was evasive. That's not out of the ordinary when you are talking to someone about someone who had been killed, but it does get your attention. He tried to pass off his answers to my questions as a joke," said Bechtol, who was a seasoned officer and sensed that Cooley was not telling him everything that he knew. At the same time, Cooley, a part-time bartender and truck driver for a transit company in Battle Creek, did not seem to have any reason to conceal information.

"I suggested that I set up a polygraph. We could then question him and clear him of any involvement. He was hesitant but agreed," Bechtol recalled. Cooley left the interview and, that night, went to a gas station three blocks from where he lived. Cooley had a key to the station and let himself in. He rode a car up on a hoist and turned it on, killing himself on the carbon monoxide fumes.

For Bechtol, it seemed to be a slam-dunk. You talk to a person about their involvement in a crime, and they kill themselves shortly thereafter, apparently to avoid taking the polygraph test. And that wasn't the lost odd occurrence: "Not too long after that, Cooley's brother tried to kill himself too. I came across him trying to commit suicide in a hayfield. He had run a hose from the exhaust into the car and left it running. He was all blue when I found him but I was able to revive him."

The fact that Albert Cooley had killed himself at the suggestion of a polygraph test seemed to be lost amid the burgeoning case file. There were good reasons for it. At the time, the young Emmett Township Police Department had not even implemented a filing system for its case notes. In fact, Bechtol had brought in his brother who worked at the Federal Center to help him organize their ever-increasing sea of paperwork. "Back then we didn't have forms, we wrote out our notes long-hand on legal pads and then filed them away," Bechtol explained. His interview with Albert Cooley didn't get cataloged with the state police until he mentioned it a year later in November 1965.

Detective Steinbacher went out to Bechtol's house to interview him. Steinbacher dug into the case. Albert Cooley had been arrested for drunk and disorderly behavior in 1959 but otherwise had a clean record. His fingerprints were on file from that arrest, and Detective Steinbacher ordered that they be forwarded to the crime lab for comparison.

The results were negative. No one thought to check the brother's fingerprints at the time. The focus in 1965 was on Albert. The question of whether Albert killed himself because he knew the crime or because he assisted with it was destined to remain unanswered for decades.

Leroy Steinbacher brought a new focus and vigor to the Zick investigation. Whereas the original investigators had gotten into a mode of only acting on tips and leads, Steinbacher went on the offensive. He began to search for possible suspects. Any acts of violence against women were checked against the Zick case. For example, when twenty-five-year-old George Herr of Grand Ledge was arrested for the murder of Betty Reynolds, Steinbacher contacted the local state police post to check Herr's fingerprints against the unidentified print from Daisy's car (though it was not a match).

While working another investigation about a Howard Schneider, who had a reputation for molesting women in the area, Steinbacher wondered if Schneider might be involved with the Zick crime. It is important to note that charges had never been raised against Schneider by the women involved, but Steinbacher began to check the man's old addresses and learned he lived in Emmett Township, not far from the Zick home. His wife, Margaret, worked at Kellogg's at the same time that Daisy did as well. Steinbacher felt this warranted further checking. He contacted Floyd Zick, who indicated that Daisy had never mentioned either one of the Schneiders. Schneider's fingerprints failed to match the print obtained from Daisy's car. While it was another blind alley, Steinbacher was, at least, keeping the case going.

———•———

For Detective Steinbacher and others on the case, two new tips came in on January 10, 1967, that raised the only person named a suspect in the Zick case. The two tips came in at roughly the same time. Virgil Pugh had been at Loravina's Bar on West Michigan Avenue, when he saw a man, William Daily, make a threat to a woman who refused to dance with him. State police trooper John Karson reached out to Detective Steinbacher and said that he had received an unconfirmed tip that William Daily had recently threatened to "do to a woman what had been done to Daisy Zick."

William Daily was no stranger to the Zick case. He had been interviewed the day of the murder since he had been Daisy's mailman. His account of that morning had been somewhat off from the others that day. First, he claimed that when he had been at the Zick home, the garage door had been down, while all other accounts had the door being open by 11:00 a.m. when he would have been there. Secondly, Daily had claimed to have seen a sullen man walking on Michigan Avenue by the Chuck Wagon that morning but was the only person that witnessed a hitchhiker in that area. Despite these discrepancies, the original investigators never bothered to follow-up with Daily to attempt to determine why his accounts were so far off.

Steinbacher spoke with another rural mailman, Rupert Hoxie, to get a feel about Daily. From what Hoxie had heard, Daily was planning on moving to Florida to look for a job. Hoxie also told Steinbacher that Daily was currently living in Springfield in a trailer park. It took some time for officers to find Daily. He had separated from his wife, Virginia, and was living with a Mrs. Cooley who lived next door to his former spouse.

Daily was finally asked to come to the state police post in Battle Creek. At 8:10 p.m. on January 6, he came in.

The forty-two-year-old Daily was not an easy man to interview, even for the seasoned Steinbacher:

> *This subject appeared to be highly emotional, very sensitive, overly talkative and somewhat nervous. Although he is noted to be a heavy drinker, did not appear to have been prior to this interview. He was informed of his constitutional rights as this interview was being conducted. He stated that on the day he noted a subject walking toward town near the Chuck Wagon restaurant about 10:10 a.m. He changed his original story in stating he thought the subject could have been a woman. When confronted with this change, states the officer must have misunderstood him. Daily being a very difficult individual to interview, as appears to be able [to] anticipate the next question. He recalled the garage door on the Zick garage as being closed as he remembers. He was asked if he had any suspects on his route that he might believe should be checked and commented he had no ideas.*

Steinbacher queried Daily as to why he was going to Florida to live and if he intended to return to Michigan to resign from the post office. He claimed that he was going down to Panama City to get employment as the manager of a nightclub. His aunt, Daisy Kennedy, was helping him secure this job.

Dick Stevens, familiar with the case from day one, was present during the interview:

> *I remember going to the Post and setting* [sic] *in an adjoining room from where Kenney was questioning him, and it seemed a couple of times he was on the verge of saying something useful and Kenney gave up and came next door. And Stein wanted to go in with the guy and not be as easy as Bob had been. Kenney vetoed any further interrogation, and we went home and mailman went to Florida.*

His reasons for leaving Battle Creek revolved around the break-up of his marriage a year earlier. Daily had a run-in with the law as a result of his divorce. When asked about his previous arrests, he described an assault charge he had received on September 28, 1966. Daily admitted that he had parked his car four blocks from his wife's dwelling and walked over to her home, breaking down the door and assaulting his wife's current suitor. For that crime, he had been fined and received a thirty-day suspended sentence. That was what he admitted to the investigators interrogating him. In reality, Steinbacher and the other officers knew that he had not gone over to assault his wife but had gone to attack his daughter-in-law that evening. The fact that he had so blatantly lied about the event was not lost on the investigators.

Daily said that he would be more than willing to take a "lie detector test," or "truth serum." Steinbacher noted that, during his interview, Daily answered every question by looking straight into his eyes and did not show any guilt reactions. At the same time, his story did not match up with some of the known facts, and it was a red flag for the officers.

William Daily said that he would be glad to take a polygraph test when he returned from Florida. His fingerprints were submitted to the crime lab but did not match those recovered from Daisy's car. It appeared, at least on the surface, that he might not have anything to do with the crime. But his inconsistencies stuck in the mind of Steinbacher. William Daily remained in the forefront of his thinking on the Zick case.

Detective Steinbacher wasn't the only officer who was probing in the chilled files of the Zick murder. His partner, Robert Kenney, was also following up on active leads. A detective of the Kalamazoo County Sheriff's department, Gilbert Kinney, said that while he was interviewing one George Worden for a parole violation for circulating a bad check, Worden had asked to meet with the Calhoun County Prosecutor in regard to the Zick case.

The new prosecutor, John Jereck, was younger than the investigators that he worked with. He had been born in 1936 and was a graduate of the University of Detroit and the Detroit College of Law. Jereck had been admitted to the state bar in 1964 and had run for the job of prosecutor that same year. While his political leanings were conservative, he ran as a Democrat. In quiet Calhoun County, the role of prosecutor was a part-time job. Jereck had hoped to win the job because it would be good on his résumé and would help his civil law practice. He rode into office in 1964 as did many Democrats, tugged in on the coattails of President Kennedy's election two years earlier. He inherited the Zick case from his predecessor, and like Kenney and Steinbacher, he wanted to see it solved on his watch.

Arrangements were made at the Kalamazoo County Jail to interview Worden about what he might know. Detective Kinney along with Detective Robert Kenney joined Jereck in the talk with the prisoner.

George Worden said that he had been involved with several breaking and entering crimes with Norman C. Baker. In May 1966, Baker had told him that he had killed someone. At the end of that month, Worden traveled from Battle Creek to Florida and stopped in Lima, Ohio, where he picked up Norman Baker for the trip south. They eventually moved into a mobile home park in Miami, Florida, along with a June McDonald.

One day, Norman had been drinking and laid down on the ground, talking and generally "running himself down." While lying there, he admitted to Worden that "he had killed the Zick woman." Baker went on to state that he had been getting money from her, and as he was hot, he went to get some money. Daisy allegedly refused and slapped him, so he got a knife out to scare her. When she slapped him again, he stabbed her. She began to scream, so he stabbed her several more times.

Baker supposedly had told Worden that he had walked to the Zick residence and had hoped to get $300 from Daisy's account at the Kellogg Credit Union. Baker had allegedly admitted to Worden that he had had an affair with Daisy, and he had been blackmailing her to call Mr. Zick at the store where he worked if she did not provide him the money.

Worden had also said that another man in jail who knew Baker might be able to offer additional information, one Arvin Davis. Davis was pulled in and admitted to meeting Norman Baker in January 1963. Both men had been sentenced to some time in Jackson State Penitentiary in May 1963.

According to Davis, Baker had talked to him about Daisy Zick as well. He said that he spoke about her continually, "stating that he knew her real well." He told Davis that he knew where she lived, that he had a girlfriend that lived on High Street and her car had been left on East Michigan Avenue on the day of the murder. Baker had also said that there had been a big storm the day that Daisy had been killed.

Detective Kenney's notes on the interview indicated that Baker had told Davis that he was extremely nervous and he wanted to get onto a prison farm so that he could escape. His fear was that the Calhoun County authorities would find out about some matters and keep him in jail for the rest of his life.

It was an amazing amount of information, but even the young prosecutor knew that jailhouse confessions were often inaccurate. While Worden's revelations about Baker killing Daisy were tantalizing, there seemed to be some gaps. Daisy did not have that kind of money in the bank on the day of the murder. The threat to tell Floyd was a hallow one that Daisy would not have been intimidated by. The sheer amount of overkill indicated someone who had a serious emotional grudge with Daisy, yet the version Worden told was of a spontaneous crime. Much of what Davis revealed, in his discussion with the investigators was information that could have been gleaned from newspaper and magazine accounts. It could have been a case of an inmate bragging to make himself seem more of a threat in jail as easily as a series of potential confessions to a murder.

Detective Kenney wasted no time. He ordered Norman Baker's fingerprints submitted to the crime lab in Lansing. They came back as not a match to the car fingerprint.

Both Steinbacher and Kenney had managed to bring new life to the Zick case. Things changed in the autumn of 1967, however, when another crime, with possible links to Daisy Zick, erupted six miles down the road from her murder scene.

The investigation of the Zick murder went onto the back burner in August 1967. A most unusual crime took place in Calhoun County's quaint town of Marshall, just a few minutes from where Daisy died. A postal bomb had been delivered to the Tasty Café on Michigan Avenue, the main street of the postcard-like city. The explosion killed one of the owners of the small diner, Nola Puyear.

Bombings in 1967 were rare and in stark contrast to the pastoral setting of Marshall. Where Battle Creek was an industrial city, Marshall was a town out of the 1950s in both appearance and culture. Both detectives Kenney and Steinbacher found themselves as lead state police investigators on the case. The bombing had sent ripples of fear throughout Calhoun County, and for the first time since 1963, a crime superseded Daisy Zick's murder in the minds of citizens.

Being a bombing, the case dealt with complex evidence and new scientific techniques for testing what had been recovered at the crime scene. Things were evolving in the state of criminal investigations, and it became clear that men like Kenney and Steinbacher were on the bleeding edge of such technologies and techniques.

After three months of investigation, an arrest was made thanks to the *Detroit News*'s Secret Witness program. The man arrested was Enoch Dalton Chism, a portly wife abuser. The bombing murder was not Chism's first brush with the law. In 1963, he had tried to burn down a rental home that his brother owned in downtown Marshall. He was a man who was violently obsessed with his wife. How he remained free of jail is a matter of some conjecture, but what was known was that Enoch Chism was more than capable of committing violent acts, including blowing another person up.

As Kenney and Steinbacher learned after his arrest, Chism had been an employee of Kellogg's from 1960 until July 30, 1966, when he was fired for drinking on the job. The first thought in the detectives' minds was that Enoch Chism was employed at Kellogg's at the same time that Daisy Zick was. More importantly, despite the in-depth sweep of the Kellogg's employees done in 1963, Enoch Chism had somehow been overlooked.

Was it possible that the bomber from Marshall might be involved with the Zick murder? If so, it would have solved two of the most publicized crimes in Calhoun County in one fell swoop. Fred Ritchie, who had worked on the Zick murder and was placed on the Chism investigation for the sheriff's office, sent a copy of Chism's fingerprints up for checking against the print found in Daisy's car. At the same time a check was made of Chism's timecard for the day of the murder to see if his time was accounted for.

Chism's fingerprints were not a match for the unidentified print from the car, and his time was accounted for the day of the murder. What also ruled out Enoch was that the crime didn't fit his modus operandi. Other than beating his wife, Chism was not a man given to direct, face-to-face attacks.

Even his use of a postal bomb was a passive way to commit a violent murder. His motive for the bombing was to force the owners of the restaurant to sell so that he could purchase it and have his wife work with him, a means of keeping her tightly under his control. His obsession with his wife simply didn't fit as any sort of scenario where he might be compelled to kill Daisy, if he had even known her.

While the Puyear murder drew in the investigators, by the end of October, they could once more turn their attention to Daisy's death. More importantly, they had two potential avenues beyond Chism to pursue. One, the postman William Daily, who seemed suspicious, had made comments to people regarding Daisy's death that seemed inappropriate at best and threatening at worse. Two, Norman Baker, had allegedly confessed his involvement to one cohort in his criminal activities and had mentioned the crime to another.

One of these two men would be ruled out as being involved. Another would be the only named suspect in Daisy's murder.

Chapter 8

THE PRISONER, THE POSTMAN AND THE EVER-CHILLING TRAIL

Everyone was talking about it because she was a Kellogg employee. She was a colorful lady, well liked at the company and very petite, and good-looking.
Detective Leroy Steinbacher
Battle Creek Enquirer and News
February 1, 1999

The bombing murder of Nola Puyear disrupted work on the Zick case. There were only so many resources that could be rallied to such a complex investigation. By December 1967, with Enoch Chism under arrest for the Puyear murder, Detective Steinbacher turned his attention back to Daisy Zick. His primary focus was the Zicks' postman, William Daily.

Detectives Steinbacher and Kenney contacted twenty-four-year-old Susan Denny. From 1962 to 1966, she had been married to James Daily, the son of William Daily. Susan had remarried, and her new husband was a member of the Battle Creek Fire Department. At the time of the murder, Susan and her then husband, James, had been living with William and his wife, Virginia.

From her memory, her father-in-law had been acting odd the day of the murder. He had mentioned seeing a man walking down Michigan Avenue by the Chuck Wagon restaurant. The mention of Daily seeing a man near the Chuck Wagon restaurant must have stood out with the detectives. In his own interview, Daily had insisted that the original officer that had taken his statement had gotten it wrong, that he had actually seen a woman. Yet in his own personal admission to his daughter-in-law, he stated that it was a man. This kind of inconsistency raised suspicions with the seasoned detectives. According to Mrs. Denny, Daily had claimed that he had not turned this information over to police—another lie. He had gone so far as to tell her that, on several occasions, he had taken a polygraph test in relation to the Zick murder, another misrepresentation, since he had moved to Florida before taking a polygraph and had never returned to Michigan for further examination.

Daisy in 1948. *Courtesy of James King.*

There was more. At one point, William Daily had made inappropriate advances toward his daughter-in-law and threatened that he knew who killed Daisy Zick. Daily had been involved with a violent clash with the Denny family. In 1966, he had broken down the door and attempted to choke Susan. During this assault, he had further charged that Susan was his wife and that her baby was, in reality, his child. The unstable Daily had claimed that Susan had been responsible for setting the police after him.

Susan had suggested that the investigators talk to a Beverly Iden who worked with William Daily. It seemed promising, but other tips came in, delaying the investigators getting to Mrs. Iden. In June 1968, they finally arranged to meet with her.

Beverly Iden had been a sub-carrier for the U.S. Mail and had worked with William Daily in 1963. When Steinbacher met with her, she was open in admitting that Daily had acted "rather odd" after the murder. She also mentioned that he had a dark-colored jacket that he wore most of the time, but after the crime, she noticed that he stopped wearing the coat altogether. The coat's style was described as being similar to an Eisenhower.

Mrs. Iden recalled that on one occasion, she and Daily had stopped at a drive-in restaurant on East Michigan Avenue for dinner. Just after they had gotten their meal, the men at the next table started talking about the murder loud enough for the two of them to overhear it. Daily, per her recollection, became upset and told her, "Let's get out of here."

On another occasion, she added, Daily had told her that he had seen Daisy Zick in the nude, taking sun baths in her backyard. Mrs. Iden told officers that she had wanted to come forward to talk to the police, but her husband held her back from making any report.

Daisy's sunbathing nude was only mentioned in the police reports in this instance, but several individuals came forward during the writing of this book to confirm these activities. Both were young boys at the time who admitted that Daisy's provocative sunbathing was the stuff of legend. As one young Zick neighbor put it, "I was fourteen years old when she lived there. We would peek through the hedge to watch her sunbathing topless. For us, this was incredible."

Detective Kenney was doing his own probing into the Zick file. He received a tip regarding Wayne Cox, an AFL-CIO Community Service Representative in Battle Creek who knew of a friend of Daisy's that might have information relevant to the case. The information was thin. Cox had dated this woman, known only as "Chelida" (spelled phonetically). He didn't know her last name. Cox had said that she claimed to be a close friend of Daisy's.

Kenney spoke with Floyd Zick, who remembered the woman. Indeed, two decades ago, Chelida and Daisy had been close friends. She had been married and divorced several times since then. He had not seen her in years and had heard that she had moved to California.

Detective Kenney reached out again to Garrett Vander Meer regarding his observations of the driver of the Zick car. For his part, Vander Meer offered no new details about the driver. Kenney had heard that Vender Meer had been in a fight with a man at the time of the murder, which he confirmed, stating that he only knew the man as Bush. Prior to the Zick murder, he had gone so far as to follow this Bush person home on Wattles Road. When Kenney pressed him, Vander Meer indicated that Bush was definitely not the person he had seen driving the car the day of the murder.

On the same day that he spoke with Beverly Iden, Detective Steinbacher received a tip on someone who had seen the murderer the day of the crime. While investigating another matter, Steinbacher met with Ed Wood, who was in the well-drilling business on the day of the murder. At just after 10:00 a.m. on the day of the crime, he was traveling south on Wattles Road, when he noticed the white Pontiac pulling onto Wattles Road from Juno Street. Mr. Wood had known Daisy Zick and knew it was her car. He had expected to see her behind the wheel. What he saw was a white male driving the Pontiac. The driver had long wavy hair that was a mix of black and gray. Most importantly, he noted that the hair had a rather odd part in it. The driver of the car was pale.

Mr. Wood had never come forward because he felt he couldn't make a positive identification and because someone had informed him that if he came forward so late after the crime, he would be in trouble with the law.

The impact of the interview was noted by Steinbacher in his notes: "The undersigned interviewed Wm. Daily on 1-8-67 and noted that his hair style is very similar to that given by Wood's in recent interview." This description also matched the description that had been provided years earlier by Vander Meer. Steinbacher and Kenney were closing in tightly on William Daily as the man that killed Daisy.

But hairstyle and flip-flopping on details of the events of that day were not enough to issue a warrant against Daily. There was more. According to one source, "My good friend Roy Steinbacher was told by a source who said he would deny telling Roy anything, that he saw the mailman driving Floyd's car North on Wattles Road." Years later in an interview with the *Battle Creek Enquirer and News*, Steinbacher seemed to confirm this account: "Steinbacher said someone he describes only as a prominent businessman told him he saw a man driving Zick's car a short distance from her home about 9:30 a.m. the day of the murder. 'He never said anything for five years because,' he said, 'I didn't want to get involved,' Steinbacher said."

With a potential witness that would not testify in court, the police were forced to continue the search for evidence that would allow a warrant. New cases in 1968 surpassed the Zick case, however, including a stabbing that took place less than a mile from where Daisy had been slain.

—·•·—

On Sunday, December 1, 1968, fourteen-year-old Nancy Marie Fleece had been shopping with her friend Deborah Lamont at Shopper's Fair on East Columbia Avenue outside of Battle Creek. Nancy was a bright young woman, always prompt and well liked. She was in the ninth grade at Southwestern Junior High and had recently won the Youth Talent Award from the *Battle Creek Enquirer and News*. Witnesses reported seeing a man in a light blue compact car accosting Nancy the day she disappeared. But other than that, Nancy had seemed to vanish from the face of the earth.

Her disappearance was punctuated four days later, when a man called the Fleece home demanding $10,000 in ransom for the young girl's return. The police waited with the Fleece family for the next call. This time the kidnapper called and said to travel to a coin-operated laundry in Ypsilanti, Michigan, and to wait for another phone call there. Detective Kenney and other officers, both in Battle Creek and Washtenaw County, mobilized in hopes that this might lead to Nancy coming home alive.

The kidnapper, thinking he was communicating with the Fleece family and they had the ransom money, instructed them to go to the nearby Huron Motor Inn. He would then collect the money, and Nancy could be found in Room 127. When the car pulled into the motor inn, a man attempted to grab $800 of ransom money from who he thought was the Fleeces. In reality, it was Detective Robert Kenney and Battle Creek detective Robert Tolf. They apprehended Russell Clayton Dodge Jr. of Ypsilanti. A sweep was made of the motor inn, only to find that room 127 didn't exist, nor was Nancy anywhere to be found.

Michigan Bell Telephone had been able to trace the long-distance call to Dodge as well. He was interrogated by detectives Kenney and Steinbacher and tried to lie his way out of the incident, claiming he had been paid to pick up the money. In reality though, it appeared that Dodge was simply taking advantage of the Fleece family in their time of greatest weakness.

The search for Nancy Fleece became a door-to-door canvassing of the neighborhood where she was last seen. Officers fanned out, trying to stir up leads and tips. After a week, however, the trail seemed to have gone cold.

Emmett Township police chief Roy Bechtol requested assistance from the Emergency Assist Radio Service CB Club from Athens–Union City. While the crime had not taken part in Emmett Township, every local law enforcement agency was pitching in to do what it could to help. Chief Bechtol asked the CB club to sweep the areas where teenagers went for moments of intimacy—namely the Ott Biological Preserve, County Park and the areas along the meandering Kalamazoo River.

County Park and the roads in that area, including Wattles Road, were well-established lovers' lanes and were quickly the focus of the search. Given the distance from where she was last seen, the search was akin to looking for a needle in the haystack, but it had to be tried. Fifty-two-year-old Roy Fredenburg of the CB Club pressed his December 12 search into a gravel pit area just a quarter mile from County Park and the river. The gravel pit was wet from a recent snowfall that had melted off and was dotted with garbage dumped by locals. He saw some dead brown leaves and crossed a tributary to the river. On the other side, he saw a small figure, maroon slacks and blue stocking–covered feet. Half buried in the gravel were the remains of Nancy Fleece.

The autopsy of Nancy indicated that she had been the victim of a knife attack. The wounds on her decomposing body revealed that her throat had been cut. She had been stabbed multiple times in the chest.

The significance of the proximity of where Nancy Fleece was found and the Zick home on Juno Street was not lost on locals. The Zicks lived within a half mile of the gravel pit where Nancy's remains had been found. Both women were the victims of knife attacks. Was it possible that after five years, the same murderer of Daisy Zick had struck again?

Nancy's case, however, was resolved relatively quickly. On Christmas Eve 1968, Jerald Dale Hall, a nineteen-year-old, kidnapped a seventeen-year-old Concord girl at knife point in downtown Albion and raped her. Hall had been arrested for the crime and, while in jail, had talked to other inmates about his murder of Nancy Fleece.

Jerald Hall's defense was woefully ill conceived on his part. Hall claimed, "I picked her up downtown. I don't remember what happened after that." He also claimed, "She took out the knife I held on her and pulled it to her. She got hysterical and pulled the knife across her throat." His story did not explain the stab wounds on Nancy's chest. Hall's defense was, in essence, that Nancy had killed herself.

Detective Steinbacher ordered Hall's fingerprints to be checked with the unidentified print in the Zick case, but there was no match. On April 24, 1970, he interviewed Hall regarding Daisy's murder. Hall knew of the crime but claimed no knowledge of Daisy's murder. Steinbacher noted, "Jerald Hall was fourteen years old at the time of the murder and information learned [was] that he was unable to drive a car at the time." Given that Daisy's car had been driven from her house, Hall proved to be a dead-end.

——•—•—•——

There were other tips that came in but only at a rate of one every year or two. The Zick case became colder with each passing day. Despite new cases for Detective Leroy Steinbacher, the Zick case never wandered far from his mind.

In July 1970, Steinbacher followed up on an earlier tip, that of former prisoner Norman Baker who had been referenced by two separate individuals as having claimed to have involvement in Daisy's death. Jailhouse bragging and confessions were always suspect in the eyes of investigators, but Steinbacher was determined to follow every lead.

Baker had been released from jail and had returned to the Battle Creek area. He met with the detective who asked if he knew George Worden, the man to whom he had allegedly confessed years earlier. "I think I know what you are getting at," he replied. Baker had said that while in prison he had heard that Worden had been talking to the police about him being the killer of Daisy Zick. Baker went on to say that he had confronted Worden about the accusation in late 1967 while in prison and claimed he had been simply making small talk. Baker went on to say that he denied making such a statement about Daisy Zick. He didn't know her personally and had only heard of the case through the local newspapers. Baker went so far as to volunteer for a polygraph test.

Five months later, Baker went to the Paw Paw Post of the Michigan State Police, where he was administered a polygraph test. There seemed to be no link between him and Daisy's murder.

Worden, however, remained adamant that Baker was connected to the murder. When George Worden was arrested again in May 1976, he contacted the sheriff's deputy, Willi Bloch, telling him that Baker had confessed the murder to him, and even more remarkably, he had been shown the shirt Baker had worn while committing the crime. This time Worden's story had a new level of depth to it. According to him, in May 1966, he had visited Baker at the house where Baker's mother lived on Fountain Street in Battle Creek.

After a few drinks, Baker had invited him to join him outside—he had something he wanted to show him. In Worden's account, "Going outside to the north-east corner of the house, Baker began digging. Baker dug up a package, which consisted for something wrapped in old newspaper." On opening the newspaper, Baker showed Worden a dark blue shirt, which had dark stains on the front. According to Worden, "Baker said that this was the shirt he was wearing when Daisy Zick fell against him while he was in her house in 1963. Baker then rewrapped the shirt in the papers and reburied it."

Ralph Kartheu, now a sergeant and one of the few original investigators still in the area, took the interview for the state police. He went to the prosecutor, James Norlander, who said that if permission to search the property from the owner could be obtained, a warrant was not necessary since Baker no longer resided there. The owner of the property gave the permission.

Worden was brought out of the county jail and showed the officers where he had seen the alleged shirt. The officers dug into the ground, but no trace of the shirt could be found. If the shirt had been there ever, it was long gone.

But the odds of it being there to begin with were fairly slim. If the shirt had been there all along, why didn't Worden mention it in his initial interview with investigators? At best, this was the case of someone hoping to implicate another man in hopes it might impact his own time in prison. After the dig, Worden was returned to the Calhoun County Jail in Marshall.

———•─•———

Detective Steinbacher never wavered in his conviction that William Daily was the man who had been seen driving Daisy's car and been her murderer. Four times in 1972 he opened the case file and twice went on the search to see if Daily had returned to the Battle Creek area so that he could speak with him. He was disappointed both times. Daily had remained in the south, moving between Florida and Alabama.

The following year, after decades of service, Leroy Steinbacher retired from the Michigan State Police. One of his last acts as the person who was most associated with the case still was to get some of Daisy's personal belongings returned to Floyd Zick. A decade after Daisy was slain, Steinbacher had her last paycheck from Kellogg's turned over to him, for the miniscule amount of $25.96, as well as the contents that had been confiscated from Daisy's locker at the plant.

Twenty-five years after his retirement, in a 1998 interview with the *Battle Creek Enquirer and News*, Steinbacher said that the Zick case was one that nagged him the most: "I have found that in any case there is always one or two or three people who know something but stay back. They don't want to get involved. Had he [the man that had said he had seen the driver of Daisy's car] come forward...

"Sometimes I wake up and make notes in the night. And if I hear something, I call the post to this date. In this old world, there is nothing more violent than a homicide. They are such a challenge, and because of the seriousness, you kind of wear them," he told reporter Trace Christenson.

With Steinbacher's retirement, the Zick case had no steward actively engaged on it for years. But it would eventually pass to another generation of investigators who would pry open the material and begin the search for the killer anew.

Chapter 9
TWILIGHT

To me, Daisy Zick is interesting because it does not fit. When you look at a crime scene, you should be able to put an individual in the place of the killer, and their actions throughout should fit like the story lines you create for a book. We all have character traits from crazy to mild. We are organized or not, smart or not, calculating or not...by these actions if you or I kill someone, you should see that character pattern throughout the scene. There are hiccups in this one. Those create questions that could be answered in at least a couple ways.
Former detective Gary Hough to the author

In May 1982, over nineteen years after the death of Daisy Zick, Mrs. DeFrance, the neighbor who had reported the sighting of a man at the door of the Zick home, received a mysterious phone call. "Is this the DeFrances'?" the male voice, sounding roughly like that of a black male, asked. Mrs. DeFrance replied, "Yes." The voice responded curtly, "A woman killed Daisy Zick."

Mrs. DeFrance was stunned. After all these years, the fear of having her name printed in the newspaper as having witnessed the murderer seemed to be coming back to roost. Stunned, she asked, "What?"

The male voice repeated his ominous message: "A woman killed Daisy Zick." Mrs. DeFrance hung up on the caller and contacted the state police. Ralph Kartheu logged the call, though there was nothing that could be done in the era before caller ID.

On the anniversary of the day of Daisy's murder in 1985, twenty-two years after her death, a two-day meeting was convened at the Michigan State

Police Post in Battle Creek. The purpose of the meeting was for investigators to go over the gathered evidence and to review the case with the purpose of possibly spotting something new or different that had been overlooked. It was also to focus on the key suspects in the case, what would now be referred to as "persons of interest." Experts would be brought in from the state police crime lab in Lansing to offer their perspectives. Twenty-two years of criminal science had passed, and it was hoped that fresh eyes might help reinvigorate the case. Former investigators, such as Ralph Kartheu and Trooper John Karstens, were brought in, as was the retired detective Steinbacher. Their experience with the case would prove invaluable to the newcomers.

The names of the "suspects" to be discussed were as follows:

Audrey Heminger: "Daisy's self-professed best friend."
William Daily: the postman.
Ray Mercer: Daisy's boyfriend.
Floyd Zick: Daisy's husband.

One of the key attendees was Lieutenant Darrell Pope. He had been brought in because of his experience with sex-motivated crimes. Pope cautioned that he had not fully reviewed the case file or all of the photographs at the time that he spoke but could offer some potential appraisal of potential suspects.

His insights were detailed as the following: "Pope did not believe the killer to be a woman because there was no mutilation of the vaginal area. Further because of the stab wounds around the left breast, he feels that the killer had a fetish for large breasts; possibly the killer's mother had large breasts. Further the killer was either separated, divorced or not married at the time of the killing. Pope stated that the killer probably didn't want to rape the victim but instead just wanted to 'look.' Lieutenant Pope advised that the following five years after the murder would be very interesting because there should be some other activity of the suspect."

One of the men sitting in on the meeting, Sergeant Lardie, had received a tip that Enoch Chism had been involved with the Zick murder. Former detective Steinbacher had submitted Chism's fingerprints, which, with his work records, had cleared him. Still, his name had been tossed out. A call was made to Kellogg's employee Jim Nelson, Chism's former supervisor. He had retired in 1984 but remembered Chism all too well. Chism had been at work the day of the crime, time clock records had shown him working his shift from eleven-to-seven, though from what Nelson remembered, Chism had come in a few minutes late the day of the murder. It was well known at

Kellogg's that it was possible to have co-workers clock you in and out if you needed to leave the plant, but there was no indication that this was the case. Chism simply didn't work in a capacity that would have brought him in close personal contact with Daisy. Per Nelson, Chism was a "loner" but a good worker who generally didn't talk to his co-workers.

Mercer, on the other hand, had a role performing repairs that left him away from visibility of his supervisor for long periods of time. Nelson advised that it was entirely possible that Mercer could leave for an hour or two and not be detected. The gathered investigators noted that Raymond Mercer was a member of the Navy CB Reserve and had prior military service with the U.S. Navy.

Nelson also knew Audrey Heminger. She used a great deal of her medical leave. Although she seemed mild-mannered, she had a very bad temper.

By the end of the first day of meetings, it was decided to recheck Enoch Chism's fingerprints and to attempt to reinterview Audrey Heminger if she would consent.

The second day's discussion focused on William Daily. The officers had attempted to contact Susan Denny, but she was ill at the time and couldn't meet with them. Daily's ex-wife, Virginia, was willing to speak with the officers.

She had not seen or heard from her former husband for some time. Daily had come to her brother's funeral. Virginia had worked at Kellogg's for a time and knew Daisy, though, by her own account, not very well. The night of the murder, when the TV news ran the story, Virginia mentioned that she had casually known Daisy from Kellogg's and she remembered her as being very meticulous. Daily had said that she was on his route and, "He had seen her when she was not so meticulous, alluding that he had seen her with next to nothing on for clothing." More interestingly, Daily had not told his wife that he had been questioned by the police regarding the crime.

Following some of the direction from Lieutenant Pope, they asked about Daily's background and relations with his mother. Virginia said that his mother was a small attractive woman with reddish-colored hair. She "had a nice figure and was well endowed." According to Daily's ex-wife, his mother weighed approximately 115 pounds. She confided to the officers that Daily and his mother didn't get along at all. His parents had been divorced when he had been a small boy, which may have contributed to their relationship issues.

When pressed about her ex-husband's attack on their daughter-in-law Susan, she claimed that she was not aware of the assault. She did reiterate that Daily had been the reason that Susan and her son James's marriage had ended. She doubted that her son would be of much help given that he had a strong dislike of his father and the two had not maintained any sort of communication.

It was clear that William Daily was becoming more of the focus of the investigators' attention. His whereabouts, per his ex-wife, had been difficult to keep track of. William Daily had become transient after leaving Battle Creek. He had lived in Indianapolis, Indiana; Panama City, Florida; Florence, Alabama; and then moved back to Panama City. From there he lived for a while in Montgomery, Alabama, before going back to Panama City. Daily then moved to Birmingham, Alabama. His jobs had ranged from managing a motel to working aboard a ship in the Gulf of Mexico.

By the end of the two days of meetings, the investigators had settled on William Newman Daily as the most likely candidate to have killed Daisy Zick. For the first time in the history of the case, there was a named "suspect." While the circumstantial evidence pointed to Daily, they still did not have enough to pursue him directly.

———•—•———

On August 7, 1988, Floyd Zick died of a prolonged illness in his home. His second wife, Doris, had passed away a year before. He had been working at the Capital Food Market until the last year of his life. The silent stares at him over the years and the whisperings about him and Daisy finally came to an end.

———•—•———

In June 1990, Detective Gary Hough of the Michigan State Police decided to clean out the closet he used at the post. In the bottom, he found a box filled with the Zick case materials. Over the years, the large box of material had likely been shuffled about the Battle Creek Post until it had unglamorously been slid into a closet.

Hough was a Michigander, raised in Grand Ledge. He joined the Michigan State Police as a cadet in 1974. He went through two recruit schools to become a trooper in 1976. Like many officers, he moved about the state in his early career, serving at the post in Jackson, Mount Pleasant, East Lansing CID/Narcotics Section and the Grand Haven Post. He came to Battle Creek as a sergeant detective in 1987.

Hough combed through the paperwork and photographs looking for some sort of hint or clue that the previous investigators may have overlooked. "The first thing I did was organize it. It was in a couple boxes of loose paper with no order to it." The case intrigued him. Hough traveled to East Lansing and went to the evidence vault that held all of the evidence related to the murder. Detective Hough reached out to Detective Marion Bagent to review all the material associated with the case. Their review of the material in the case file differed from the earlier reviews in that both of them felt that a female had been responsible for the murder.

When January 1991 rolled around, Hough decided that the time had come to forward a new theory and hope that after all the time that had passed, someone might come forward with new information.

Just a few days before the twenty-seventh anniversary of Daisy's murder, Hough granted an interview with the *Battle Creek Enquirer and News*. "We believe it's solvable, even though it's twenty-seven years old. We just never clicked on the proper suspect."

According to his analysis, Hugh believed that the murderer was a woman. There was some relatively sound basis for that logic: "It was 1963, [detectives] could not bring themselves to believe a woman could do it." He went on to validate his thinking: "[The killer] literally could not control her with her hands tied." He asserted that a stronger male would have been able to control Daisy. Hough went on to state that Zick's stab wounds were not defensive thrusts as a man would make.

He noted that Daisy had multiple affairs, which may have provided the murderer with a motive. "It was possible that the murderer could be the wife or girlfriend of one of the men with whom Zick had an affair."

While he acknowledged that Mrs. DeFrance had believed she had seen a man, it was possible that it was a woman. While he did not mention the eyewitness accounts of Mr. Vander Meer or Mr. Wood, he did concede that the hairstyle that the murderer had was more attuned to a female's hairstyle at the time.

To further booster his point, he referenced the fact that a taxicab had picked up a female in the Emmett Township area the day of the crime and had driven her to the Post Tavern. In the official case files, this woman was never identified. (Note: In the interview given to *True Detective*, the investigators said they had tracked down this woman and had cleared her.)

Detective Hough also pointed out that Mrs. DeFrance, who he tactfully did not name, had been receiving telephone calls as late as the 1980s from someone affirming that a woman had killed Daisy.

There would be challenges if the case where to be brought to trial. Many of the people who could testify were still alive, as were some of the investigators, though they were retired in most cases. The case presented frustrating angles even for seasoned investigators: "It's too bad. It looks like a one-shot emotional-type killing. The killer probably never committed a crime before that, and probably hasn't after either."

Detective Hough's appeal for public information did generate some leads. A woman working at Ralston's in Battle Creek came forward about a friend who had talked with a woman who claimed she had killed Daisy Zick. The woman was one Winnie Lutz. Tracking down the people involved with this third-hand information took several weeks.

The lead turned out to be less than useful. According to one of the people involved with the rumor chain, Winnie Lutz was a person prone to making up false stories. A check was made, and Mrs. Lutz had spent time at the Kalamazoo State Hospital. Detective Hough and Trooper William Ford interviewed her former husband and asked if it were possible that Winnie believed he had been having an affair with Daisy. Her husband admitted that she had accused him of sleeping with Daisy, but he added that she had also accused him of having an affair with his own daughter "and every other woman she could think of."

When Winifred "Winnie" Lutz came back to Battle Creek for a visit, the officers met with her. She stated that she knew her ex-husband had been "involved" with Daisy and that he had something to do with her demise. Winnie had worked at Kellogg's at the time Zick was employed there but had not worked near her in the plant.

Ultimately this lead went nowhere. There were far too many inconsistencies and counter-allegations, none of which made sense. The investigators did not rule Winnie Lutz out but did not pursue it any further.

Gary Hough was not a man who let go easily. Going back to the case file, he focused on the females who had been connected with the case over the years. In doing so, he was drawn to reinterview Minnie Smith. Smith had been closely associated with Raymond Mercer prior to Daisy's affair with him. On the day of the murder, she had withdrawn all of her money from the Kellogg Credit Union and left town.

The Michigan State Police sent Harry Zimmerman down to Florida to meet with Smith again. Smith denied that she had been having an affair with Mercer, saying that they were just good friends. She claimed that she didn't know Daisy, other than she worked on the third floor of the Kellogg's plant.

According to Smith, Raymond Mercer had been seeing Daisy for some time before the two of them had stopped driving to work together. Mercer would take off work early and ask for Smith's car keys so that he could leave Kellogg's and see Daisy before returning to pick Minnie up when she got off work.

In regard to her departure on the day that Daisy died, Minnie stood fast that she did not know that Daisy had been killed until after she had left town, when a friend had written to her about the murder.

The article in the newspaper had stirred up a handful of new leads but nothing that went anywhere. One lead that came in suggested that a lesbian may have been involved with Daisy and been the killer. This lead, when tracked down, proved to be another disappointing blind alley.

Hough also reached out to Audrey Heminger. She penned a letter back to him offering little:

> *It is nice to think someone may be able to solve Daisy Zick's death. She was a very dear friend of mine; and you are right, it will be very difficult for me to go over any part of the case with anyone.*
>
> *About five years ago another Det. from the State Police came to our home, and said he was reviewing the case. He was from Fla. He said had he been on the case at the start he would have had me take a polygraph test. Not any of the former investigators thought this was necessary. All the officers, except one, who is [an] attorney in BC treated me with great respect and kindness. They even had a picture of Daisy enlarged, and gave it to me.*
>
> *Since the death of my husband, I go to pieces easy, but will do my best to try and answer any question I am able to.*
>
> *I don't plan on being back in Mich 'til late April.*

Audrey's postscript was that of a friend who was not resisting the police at all:

> *I wish you success and may God guide you.*

Today Gary Hough is retired in the Upper Peninsula of Michigan. While he admits he is not the best person to speak about the case, upon reviewing the file again, he offered his perspective as to what happened and why the case is so baffling:

The killer arrived at the Zick house in the morning at about 9:00 a.m. to 9:30 a.m. and was gone probably by 10:30 a.m. It was a cold bitter morning, so the first question you ask is how he or she got there. I do not think they walked. They were dropped off or lived within eyesight of the house. One of the reasons I do not think they were dropped off is I believe it would have come out in the investigation. The crime scene speaks to one. The car was taken from the residence.

The window near the breezeway in the bedroom would have allowed the killer to view Daisy. When Audrey Heminger called on the phone, the killer would have heard her on the phone talking with Daisy. This explains why the murderer cut the phone cord when he entered the home, to avoid the risk of being caught. It was a matter of control and apparent planning. Hugh added more:

One of the big unknown questions in this is did the killer bring the knife or take one from the kitchen. If the knife is brought it shows more of the calculating mind. Planning the whole thing. Did the killer come to talk...or kill? Is the killing secondary to something else? Is the knife part of the attack or simply something the killer picks up in the kitchen to cut the phone line? If you picked it up in the kitchen and you want to kill, why not a big old butcher knife?

The small pool of blood in the bedroom indicates that Daisy was stabbed there or in the kitchen. She was tied up, again pointing to a murderer seeking to exercise control. Hugh prepositioned: "Why tie her? It is a control thing. Look at how much control is going on by the killer up to now. The killer is standing there with a knife in his or her hand. Think about this for a second. It is great you have a knife to control the victim. It is bad because you have something in your hand that limits your use of that hand."

Daisy made a break for the spare bedroom. Once there she was stabbed again. Sliding down along the wall, someone knelt over her body and savagely stabbed at her, concentrating on her left breast.

Hough points out that the murder scene usually tells a story that helps you focus the investigation. Daisy's murder scene is a hodge-podge of contradictions:

The stabs to her back indicate a left-handed killer, but on her front, a right-handed killer. I favor left-handed because it is more natural that these thrusts were done in the spur of the moment, as she was running away from her killer…

The position of the cuts to her back indicates someone that is around five feet seven inches tall. The murder scene tells you that much. Those wounds were not deep. It was someone what wasn't very strong. Add in the tying of her hands, and you are looking at someone weak—a woman in my mind. Look at the purse. A man would have dumped the contents out of a purse, this killer doesn't. Again, this points to a woman. This kind of information can go a long way in narrowing your list of suspects.

The crime scene story does not help narrow the suspects much beyond this. "There's evidence of control here. The cutting of the phone lines, tying up the victim, etc.." "The killer goes to the kitchen and cleans up. They do it because they fear being seen with blood on them. This means they expect to be seen by someone. The control again. Not panic." "Control is lost though at the end when the killer is stabbing her over and over on the floor."

Hough's view was that this was a discussion that got out of hand: "I tend to favor that this was a confrontation that got out of hand. Otherwise why not bring a weapon with you? This killer took a knife out of the sink. Again, the scene of the crime doesn't give us a good consistent story."

Ultimately, looking back at the case over the decades, Hough drew his own conclusion: "The scene points to the possibility of it being a woman. The whole world is looking for a man in [1963]. All questions are pointed in that direction. A person would remember dropping off a man near the house on the day of the murder. Would a person bring up the fact they dropped off a woman? Women killers were simply unheard of at this time."

In 1999, Kellogg's closed its main plant facility in Battle Creek and dismantled the redbrick facility. As iconic as the plant and its highly popular public tours were, it was one more link to Daisy Zick that disappeared with time.

Despite the efforts of Detective Hough to breathe new life into the case, it once more went cold. Gary Hough went on to head up the successful investigation into the murder of Diana King, a news anchor of Battle Creek's Channel 41 who had been shot by her husband in Marshall. For the public at large, the Zick case was something still talked about but became a distant memory. The crime rate in Battle Creek rose. The heydays of part-time prosecutors came to an end, as did the era of cases always being closed. More cold cases appeared on the books, like the 1969 strangulation murder of Diana Lynn Black. The green-eyed, redheaded, shy and introverted fourteen-year-old freshman at Lakeview High School had run away from home a week earlier. Her partially clad body was found in a bushy area between Apperson Road and South Twenty-fourth Street. One of her shoes was off. One of her stockings had been used to strangle her. Diana Black's murder remains an open cold case still in Calhoun County.

In the late 1960s, a new kind of murder unfolded in mid-Michigan, a serial killer. In the Ann Arbor and Ypsilanti area along I-94, young coeds were being murdered with chilling frequency. In 1969, John Norman Collins was apprehended for the Coed Killer murder spree. Compared to such large-scale murders, the Zick case seemed oddly out of place.

From the public's perspective, the Zick case had been shelved. In reality, it had not been forgotten by the Michigan State Police. Detective Bill Ford kept a watchful eye on the lone suspect, William Daily, in hopes that he would return to Michigan so that he could be questioned.

In January 2000, Daily became hospitalized for cancer. With so many of the witnesses dead or their memories failing, the odds of bringing anyone to trial without a confession seemed fleeting. There was a chance, however, to close the case, if not bring someone to trial. With Daily in the hospital, still-interested detectives believed if they didn't get him interviewed, they might never have a chance to bring closure to the case.

Detective Ford opted to go to Florida to attempt to get a confession from Daily before he died. He took with him Lieutenant Lowridge, a skilled polygraph operator, with him. They arrived in Florida and met with Daily, who refused to undergo an examination, even one that could clear his name. The two investigators came back empty-handed.

Daily didn't die in 2000 from his illness. He passed away eleven years later in April 2011. With his death, the only named suspect of Daisy's murder faded away. That did not mean that the theories around her death died. In Battle Creek, the myths and potential theories around Daisy's death still emerge even today.

Chapter 10
THE MYTHS AND THEORIES

This case is unlike most murder cases.

Detective Charlie Conn
True Detective
May 1964

When you start writing a book on an unsolved crime, people come forward with their theories as to what happened, who committed the murder and potential motives. Some come in the form of outright tips, people reaching out saying, "Let me tell you what I heard happened..." Other people simply offer their speculation. With a crime that is this old, often what you get is in the form of hearsay. Some of the ideas are completely off the wall, but this *is* an open murder case. There is always a chance that one of them will solve the case.

There are certain myths that have emerged about Daisy over the years, rumors that people have simply assumed were the truth. I have opted to include them here as well. With five decades of separation between us and the crime, there is a possibility that a kernel of truth exists in even the whispered gossip tied to the case and the victim.

I'm an author and historian, not a detective. It is odd that people would reach out to me with their ideas as opposed to the police. But the leads that were credible, I shared with the Michigan State Police. Who knows, perhaps one of them will lead to this case being closed once and for all.

As people opened up to me, I found that many people wanted to see the Zick case closed as much as I did. They wanted to tell their stories so that perhaps Daisy's family could have some closure. So here are the theories and ideas that good people suggested.

MYTH

Daisy Was Killed Because of Her Little Black Book

The story of her little black book is one of the most prevalent stories told about Daisy. In interviewing several people who worked at Kellogg's at the time, this was accepted to be the motive for her demise.

This story has been conveyed to me so much that I assumed there was a source for it, a newspaper article or news report that planted the seed in the public consciousness. I was never able to find that source. It appears to be a rumor that took on a life of its own.

The root of this story is that Daisy maintained a little black book of the men that she slept with, married men. She was allegedly using the information about her affairs to blackmail her former suitors. One of these victims had her killed to recover the black book and end the blackmail. In a variation of this rumor, Daisy was sleeping with several high-ranking men in the corporate hierarchy at Kellogg's, and one of them had her killed as a result of the extortion.

This rumor was circulated to the original investigators on the case. If Daisy had been extorting money, there would have been money somewhere—in a bank account or in the house. The Zicks were a hard-working couple but lived almost paycheck to paycheck. The money in their bank accounts totaled did not amount to more than a few hundred dollars.

The investigators received a tip that Daisy had purchased some expensive watches and jewelry. The police checked, and in 1959, she had purchased a watch for $221 for herself and one that was $79 for Floyd. But other than this, the Zicks did not take expensive trips, drive pricy automobiles or have any other baubles one might have if Daisy had been on the receiving end of bribes. It is hard to conceive that someone would consider killing her over a paltry $300 in watches.

Besides leaving a money trail, for the extortion myth to be true, there would have had to be people coming forward and claiming that Daisy was indeed extorting money. There was one individual who came to the authorities in 1963. Loretta Smith was contacted by the investigators and seemed to add the only credible weight to the story. By Ms. Smith's account, Daisy had extorted money from her years earlier. However, Smith's whereabouts during the time of the murder had been verified by work records, and she was cleared.

Furthermore, Floyd Zick noted that the only missing item from his wife's purse was forty-five dollars. No mention of a black book was ever made by anyone who knew Daisy.

MYTH

Daisy's Extramarital Affairs Led to Many Divorces After Her Death

Daisy was an outgoing and fun-loving woman; this is undeniable. The public constantly referred to the vast number of affairs that she had, including with senior people at Kellogg's. In reality, the police and this author only found four men that Daisy dated while married to Floyd. Ralph Kartheu pointed out in his interview with the author: "No one wanted to admit they slept with Daisy—that would put them under a microscope." Gary Hough offers a more holistic perspective: "Everyone's a saint once they're dead."

As one person close to the case put it to me, "Daisy did fool around on her husband, but we found that she generally was only seeing one person at a time." In my digging, I found that there was an exception to that. While seeing Raymond Mercer, Daisy had at least one other affair. But this does not make her promiscuous or make her affairs "numerous."

For the most part, the stories of Daisy's extramarital affairs have been exaggerated. As to the allegations that the investigation into her murder broke up numerous marriages at Kellogg's, there doesn't seem to be any supporting evidence of this. The investigation was bound to cause some marital strife, but there are no names associated with this myth.

In reality, divorces happened in Battle Creek just like they did in every town in America. If it happened to be a person at Kellogg's, people drew assumptions that it might be connected in some way to the Zick case. It became an enduring part of the myth of Daisy Zick, one that had no connection at all to her.

MYTH

Daisy's Vocal Chords Were Ruptured from Screaming

This myth surfaced twice during the research on this book and is one of the more bizarre myths. According to two individuals I spoke to, Daisy's autopsy revealed that she had screamed so hard that she had ruptured her vocal cords. Having reviewed the autopsy report summary, I found no evidence that this happened. What is strange is that this rumor has been accepted as truth.

One variant of this is that there were children who had been walking to school at the time of the murder that morning and heard the screams. Children *did* walk past the Zick home on their way to school; however, school had been in session for hours by the time of her death. There were no children or anyone else reported that heard these alleged screams.

THEORY

Floyd Zick Killed Daisy

The police focused a great deal of attention on Floyd Zick from the moment they arrived at the Zick home. The investigators had good reason to look closely at Floyd. His wife was having affairs, after all. Jealously could be a powerful motive. When investigators spoke to Daisy's sister, Dorothy Wright, about who she would look at, she suggested that "the husband should be questioned further."

Floyd's time that day was well accounted for. He took a car pooler with him to work, and his time at Fales' Market was fully validated. Furthermore, Floyd took a polygraph voluntarily and passed. If the test was accurate, he didn't kill his wife or know who had killed her. Daisy didn't have a life insurance policy, ruling that out as a possible motive. His wife's affairs were a potential motive, but most individuals associated with the case felt that Floyd had been aware of Daisy's extramarital activities for some time. If he did kill her, what could his motive have been?

This theory refuses to die despite the evidence showing that Floyd had no involvement. I was contacted by an anonymous source, a retired seventy-nine-year-old deputy from the Calhoun County Sheriff's Department who would only talk under the condition of not having his name revealed.

At the time of the case, this informant was with the Battle Creek police department but was not attached to the case. His suspicions around Floyd were intriguing:

> *Floyd was seeing a girl over on Calhoun Street. I saw him going to visit her several times, and it was well known in town.*
>
> *He and Daisy had a gay living with them, a little guy named Ralph Hartom. He was short with dark hair. Ralph was an organist in several restaurants in town.*
>
> *Here's how it went down. Floyd killed Daisy before he went to work. He was a butcher so the blood would have not been out of place on his clothing. He put an electric blanket on her body and turned it up. Doing that would make it appear like she died later (keeping the body warm and confusing the time of death). If you look at the crime scene photos you will see an electric warmer blanket on the floor near her body.*
>
> *He [Floyd] called Ralph. Ralph was who was seen going into the house by the neighbor. All he did, at Floyd's bidding, was remove and unplug the blanket. Floyd then came home and claimed to find her dead.*

The informant passed on this tip to Prosecutor Noble Moore, but Moore "rejected it because he and Floyd were close friends."

This theory is intriguing, but the physical evidence does not substantiate it. Under this theory, Daisy was dead all morning. Yet we know that Daisy prepared her lunch and made several phone calls that morning before her demise.

There was no electric blanket at the foot of the Zick bed either. Also, there was ample evidence in the house of a struggle. If Daisy had been dead the entire morning, how did blood spatter appear in the master bedroom and the guest bedroom? Why cut the telephone cord? At the end of the day, this theory doesn't hold water.

But there is an intriguing angle to it, namely Ralph Hartom's participation. Hartom was interviewed years later in regard to the bartender at the Chuck Wagon being named as a potential suspect. While Mr. Hartom did deny that he knew Daisy, he had been raised in Assyria Township, the same small community that she had been raised in. Hartom *did* admit that he had stayed at the Zick home at that time. Ralph Hartom had never had his fingerprints tested against the one unidentified print taken from Daisy's Pontiac.

In 2013, I submitted Hartom's name to the Michigan State Police for potential fingerprint testing. While he died in the 1970s, if his prints are on file, they can be compared to the print at the crime scene.

THEORY

Albert Cooley or Someone Close to Him Was Responsible for Daisy's Murder

Roy Bechtol believes to this day that he interviewed Daisy Zick's killer just before he killed himself. Albert Cooley's death in January 1964 certainly looks suspicious. For someone to kill himself after a police interview that was going to lead to a polygraph test appears to connote some guilt.

But the investigators checked Albert Cooley's fingerprints against their one unidentified print, and it wasn't a match. After that, they stopped looking at him as a potential suspect. It is possible, however, that Cooley had taken his life because he had helped the killer or knew who the killer was. He was, perhaps, protecting someone close to him, such as his brother, who also attempted suicide a short time later. The connection could be tenuous or could prove worthy of investigation.

I have passed this information on to the Michigan State Police—for them to check fingerprints of individuals potentially associated or related to Albert Cooley. At the time of this writing, there has been no change in the status of this tip.

THEORY

Norman Baker Killed Daisy

The testimony of prisoners is always questionable at best, but the case of George Worden's finger-pointing at Norman Baker warrants some checking against facts. Worden claimed that Baker killed Daisy because she would not write him a check for $300. To begin with, the Zicks simply didn't have that kind of cash. Secondly, no explanation was provided for why Baker walked to the Zicks home.

Also Worden's rendition of Baker's account of the attack didn't match the evidence of Daisy's death. He did not mention the tying of Daisy's hands behind her back or the cutting of the telephone cord. Worden's later account of a shirt buried outside Baker's mother's residence also did not hold up.

Baker's fingerprints did not match the print found on Daisy's car, which was how he was initially cleared, followed with a polygraph. Chances are this was a case of either a prisoner bragging to other convicts to raise his stature in prison or an informant hoping to reduce his sentence by accusing another prisoner of a crime he didn't commit.

THEORY

The Mystery Man at Kellogg's Killed Daisy

During the course of writing this book, I received two tips that may or may not be related. Unfortunately, neither one came with a name attached to it.

The first was from a Battle Creek woman who claimed that her neighbor's mother knew who had killed Daisy. It was allegedly a man who worked at Kellogg's who was either asked to quit or was fired around the time of Daisy's death. This man warned several Kellogg's employees that if they talked about his involvement, he would kill them. He moved away from Battle Creek to either Arizona or Florida.

The second account came in during a telephone interview I was doing on the case on WBCK in Battle Creek. The man who called in claimed that his father knew who had killed Daisy. The man had been seen the day of the murder in the rail yard at the Kellogg's plant, washing the blood off his clothing. He warned the witness to not say anything under force of threat.

After five decades, these kinds of tips are likely to be the way that leads come in on such a murder. Kellogg's was clearly the principle focus of the early investigation. Hundreds of employees were questioned, fingerprinted and, in a few cases, polygraphed. It is certainly possible that the true killer managed to slip past that dragnet at the plant.

The second account has one potentially fatal flaw, which is that of the man cleaning himself (presumably with water) the day of the crime. The cold would have made such a cleaning effort downright painful. Additionally, more private and convenient places to wash away blood were probably available.

THEORY

The Killer Was a Jealous Woman

Detective Hough makes a compelling case for this theory. The size and strength of the murderer point to someone who had challenges controlling Daisy in the home the morning of the murder.

The only woman seriously considered at all by investigators in the days after the killing was Audrey Heminger. There was a rumor prevalent at the time that Audrey and Daisy were "competing" with each other over suitors at Kellogg's. Audrey managed to avoid her detailed interrogation by storming out of the state police post. She was fingerprinted, however, and her fingerprints did not match the print recovered from the car. At the same time, there is no way to know for sure if that print came from the murderer. Audrey was never tested with a polygraph as part of the investigation.

The biggest thing pointing away from Audrey or any other woman committing the crime is the eyewitness accounts of Mr. Vander Meer who said he saw a man behind the wheel of the Zick car, as did Mr. Wood. While someone bundled up for cold weather could be mistaken for the wrong sex, both of these witnesses said they saw a man driving Daisy's Pontiac.

THEORY

The Postman, William Daily, Killed Daisy

There is a collection of circumstantial evidence pointing to William Daily. If Leroy Steinbacher's informant was correct, Daily had been seen driving Daisy's car at the time of the murder. Daily's description of the garage door was incorrect, as he claimed it was closed when it was left open. He changed his story about a man walking near the Chuck Wagon the day of the crime, telling police in later years that it was a woman. Daily's rather unique hairstyle for the times matched the descriptions of the witnesses who saw the murderer driving Daisy's car. Daily owned a dark blue coat, matching the description that Mrs. DeFrance gave of the man at the Zick door that morning, a coat that he stopped wearing after the murder.

There were other threads that point to Daily. His threat to Susan Denny mentioning Daisy's name; the fact that he was interviewed by police the day of the crime but he didn't tell his wife about it; and the fact that he admitted that he saw Daisy sunbathing in the nude. Perhaps the biggest red flag with Daily is that he left town before he could be given a polygraph and refused to take one in 2001.

Daily's job gave him good camouflage for being in the neighborhood the morning of the murder. It would have also given him a pretext for knocking and entering the home. There's additionally the chilling description of Daily's relationship with his mother, another buxom redhead, who he had bad relations with.

Motive is not required to be presented in murder trials in Michigan, but any prosecutor will tell you that most juries need to hear it. Daily's motive to kill Daisy seems to be missing, though there are many that could be construed.

William Daily was the only person ever tagged as a suspect by the authorities in the Zick murder. If he took his secret to his grave, we may never know the truth.

THEORY

It Was Someone Else

The police could have passed over a suspect unknowingly. It may even be possible that someone who was never investigated killed Daisy. Many suspects were cleared based on the fingerprint recovered in the victim's car. While unlikely, it is possible that the fingerprint had nothing to do with the murderer. And while many potential suspects were ruled out because of successful polygraph tests, even polygraphs are not infallible.

The brutality and savagery of this crime has yet to be paralleled in Calhoun County. It seems possible that the killer moved to another part of the country, where his crimes would not be linked to Battle Creek.

Ultimately, the reality is that the killer of Daisy Zick may yet be alive.

EPILOGUE

A task force was formed for this investigation. It is a great thing in that it allows you to send a lot of bodies out to gather a lot of information. It is a bad thing in that you make the assumption that all the officers participating have the same abilities. Good investigators have the ability to, in most cases, talk to a person and through conversation determine if that individual is being truthful. People call it "gut instinct," "sixth sense," etc. Every good homicide detective I have known has it.
Gary Hough to the author
2013

As a writer, I believe in going where the evidence takes me rather than coming in with a preconceived notion and forcing the evidence to fit that belief. When I started this project two years before its publication, I was not sure what I would find. Like many people from the Battle Creek area, I knew more about the myths surrounding the crime than the facts. As I interviewed, read and did my research, I learned more than I ever anticipated both about my hometown and myself.

Some people I interviewed had an attitude about Daisy, even after five decades. There was a hint of, "She was a loose woman," as if that justified what happened to her. Whatever Daisy's private life, no one deserves what happened to her in January 1963. In talking with the few investigators who are still alive, I certainly didn't get that feeling. While her affairs may have made it a more complicated investigation, all voiced that they wanted a killer brought to justice.

The Zick home the day of the murder, as it would have appeared as the murderer approached it. *Courtesy of the Michigan State Police.*

This is still an open case with the Michigan State Police. The evidence is sealed in a vault in East Lansing, silently waiting a trial that may or may not come. While funds have been dramatically cut for investigating cold cases, these old cases are never ignored. If new tips come in, they are investigated and pursued. A new generation of detectives has taken up the mantle passed on to them by their predecessors and seeks to bring closure to this case.

People have asked if DNA testing could help close this case. It is possible, if and only if the murderer left behind any blood in the assault. But for the testing to work, you need suspects to test your findings against. All the potential persons of interest are dead now. Digging up a half dozen interned bodies would require more than a hunch—it would require a credible tip.

Fifty years takes a toll on a community, and Wattles Park is no exception. The crossroads of Wattles and East Michigan Avenue, which was the seedling for a business community in the 1960s, is now a row of empty lots and abandoned businesses. Emilio's Mexican Restaurant is a barren lot. Steve's Grocery closed, moving across the street to be the Wattles Park Grocery. Gone are the hardware and electrical businesses, replaced by empty buildings waiting for an economic boom that seems too distant.

County Park has become Bridge Park, the old bridge now part of a walkway. Wattles Park Junior High—a block from the Zick home—opened, flourished and then was closed, the throngs of expected students in the area never fully materializing. The elementary school has still managed to stay operational, a cornerstone in the area.

Where Daisy's car was abandoned in front of Sharon Brown's home is still recognizable, but the surrounding area has changed. Pine Knoll Golf Course has become apartments and fast food establishments. The Dog 'n Suds has changed hands and businesses several times, turning from restaurant to dental office, beauty parlor to convenience store. The Sandstone Motel is gone, replaced with an ice cream shop. The Chuck Wagon is a barbershop and a John Deere dealership.

One hundred Juno Street still is there. Trees and shrubs that have grown tall now mark the passage of time. The house stoically sits back on the lot, not revealing the secrets that its walls hold. It is a quaint little home, in stark contrast to the violence that took place there five decades earlier.

What is amazing is that the mention of the Zick case, even today, seems to energize people. It is like a time machine in some respects. People step forward when it is spoken about, offering their views, theories and perspectives. Because it has remained unsolved, the intrigue of the murder remains. People want to see the case resolved. If nothing else, they want to know if a killer lurked in their community for the last half century.

Ultimately, it is this concern, the fear that the murderer might have been a neighbor or even a friend, that lingers. There is no indication that the killer struck again despite the fact that he has escaped justice up to this point. People want answers, and Daisy Zick most certainly deserves it.

Someone out there holds that bit of information that can allow officials to close this case. They saw something, gave someone a lift the day of the crime, were confessed to, came across a ring of keys or found a bloody pair of gloves. It is hard to believe that the murderer was able to keep this quiet for so much time. This case will most likely never go to trial, but it can be resolved. All that is needed is for a person to shed themselves of the guilt of silence they have carried all of these years.

And so, I now need to turn to you, the reader of this book, to help solve this murder. You have the material in your hands from the case file and from the long hours of interviews I've conducted. You have seen the photographs of the crime scene. If you love a good mystery, this is one. I now have to rely on you to read the book and perhaps surface your own tips and leads.

The witnesses are almost all gone now. If the killer is still alive, he (or she) would be in his eighties. The reality is that this case may not go to trial, but new tips or leads may allow the police to finally close it. Someone saw something that day—a blood-soaked glove, a splatter of blood on someone's pants or someone hitchhiking along the road. Perhaps a relative came across a ring of keys that seemed out of place, or noticed someone behaving erratically when Daisy's name was mentioned. Just because fifty years have gone by, that doesn't mean that a resolution is impossible.

Floyd Zick is gone. Most of the witnesses are dead and buried. But Daisy's son, Jim, is still alive, and if nothing else, he deserves answers.

As a writer, I've done my part. It's now in your hands.

TIMELINE

January 14, 1963

Note: Timing is as presented in police interviews and does not always correlate.

7:45 a.m.: Floyd Zick leaves home for Fales' Market, picking up Florence Van Uun on the way.

9:00 a.m.: Floyd calls Daisy at home. She is getting ready to take a bath.

After 9:00 a.m.: Raymond Mercer calls Daisy at home.

9:15–9:20 a.m.: Daisy calls Irene Taylor at Battle Creek Health Care.

9:30 a.m.: Mae Tolls notices the Zicks' drapes are pulled open.

10:00 a.m.: Audrey Heminger calls Daisy.

10:00 a.m.: Mrs. DeFrance notices the murderer standing in front of the Zicks' breezeway.

Just after 10:00 a.m.: Ed Wood notices the Zick Pontiac turning off Juno Road onto Wattles Road. The driver is not Daisy.

10:05 a.m.: Postman William Daily claims he sees a man walking down East Michigan Avenue near the Chuck Wagon Restaurant. He is the only person who sees this alleged hitchhiker. His description changes from a man to a woman over time.

10:20 a.m.: Mrs. DeFrance sees the Zick garage door open and the car missing.

Around 10:30 a.m.: Garrett Vander Meer is behind the Zick car on East Michigan Avenue and gets a good look at the driver (a man) who is slowing down westbound traffic.

After 10:30 a.m.: While transporting a prisoner to court, Sergeant Fred Ritchie sees the Zick car on East Michigan Avenue and notices a man walking away from it.

Between 10:30 and 11:00 a.m.: Sharon Brown notices the Zick Bonneville parked in front of her home.

11:10 a.m.: Postman Daily claims that he goes by the Zick home and that the garage door is closed.

Between 11:20 a.m. and 11:30 a.m.: Mrs. Beulah Hankey claims to have passed the Zick car on Wattles Road. Chances are this sighting is off, time-wise.

12:30 p.m.: When Daisy does not show up for their lunch or at work, Audrey calls the Zick home and gets no answer.

12:30 p.m.: Audrey contacts Floyd Zick and alerts him that Daisy has not showed up to work. He leaves for his home. On the way, he spots his wife's car on Michigan Avenue and checks it. There is no sign of Daisy.

1:10 p.m.: Floyd Zick arrives at his home and finds the garage door open. A search of the house leads him to finding Daisy's body, and he contacts his manager at Fales' Market who contacts the police.

1:20 p.m.: Ralph Kartheu arrives at the murder scene. The investigation into Daisy's death begins.

INDEX

ABOUT THE AUTHOR

Blaine Pardoe is an award-winning author of numerous books in the science fiction, military nonfiction, true crime, paranormal and business management genres. Mr. Pardoe was raised outside Battle Creek, Michigan, and received his undergraduate and graduate degrees from Central Michigan University. Pardoe has been a featured speaker at the U.S. National Archives, the United States Navy Museum and the New York Military Affairs Symposium. He was awarded the State History Award in 2011 by the Historical Society of Michigan for his book about Michigan aviator Fred Zinn (*Lost Eagles*) and, in 2013, was the Michigan Aviation Hall of Fame recipient of the Harriet Quimby Award. He currently resides in Virginia outside Washington, D.C.